YOU CAN SEE THE ANGEL'S BUM,
MISS WORSWICK!

YOU CAN SEE THE ANGEL'S BUM, MISS WORSWICK!

Mike Harding

Illustrations by Banx

ARROW BOOKS

Arrow Books Limited
62-65 Chandos Place, London WC2N 4NW

An imprint of Century Hutchinson Ltd

London Melbourne Sydney Auckland
Johannesburg and agencies throughout
the world

First published by Robson Books Ltd 1985
Arrow edition 1986

Printed and bound in Great Britain by
Anchor Brendon Limited, Tiptree, Essex

ISBN 0 09 948240 1

CONTENTS

1
Life In A Catholic Air-Raid Shelter

Two things happened in 1944 to ruffle the still waters of life in our air-raid shelter. One was my birth, the other was the suicide of General Rommel in the Western Desert. My birth was a total surprise to my Grandmother who thought that my Mother was just getting fat because she was allergic to dried eggs. When my Mother came in from the night with me in her arms my Grandmother, who was from Dublin, threw down the Catholic Truth Society pamphlet she was reading, *What the Saints Ate for Breakfast,* and cried, 'In de name of God, Eileen, not another puppy to piddle on de rug!'

'It's a baby,' said my Mother.

'Do ye tell me dat now? And where would ye get such a class of yoke as dat?'

'The ack-ack crew shot down a stork, and it was carrying this in its beak.'

'Begob now, things is gettin' to a sorry state when dem

anti-aircraft boys can't tell the difference between a stork and a German bomber. Before you know it, dey'll be shootin' down de Holy Archangels of de Lord God Himself, and dey goin' about deir lawful business.'

'Mother, you're exaggerating!'

'Begob, I know I am, but it's early in the book yet and de grandson wants dem to carry on readin'.'

When news of Rommel's suicide reached our air-raid shelter, my Grandmother refused to believe it.

'Yez can't trust dem Germans. Dat class of man is a foxy manner of individual altogether. Yer man Rommel won't be dead at all. He'll be on a boat to Brazil or Peru, or somewhere of dat class, to run a rhubarb plantation in the Mato Grosso. He'll only have pretended to shoot himself. He'll have pressed de trigger, and when he heard de bullet comin' he'll have ducked.'

My Grandmother had never trusted Germans since a stray incendiary bomb intended for the Crumpsall Cream Cracker Factory had burnt the chip shop in our street to the ground.

'Begob, wasn't I out all night wid de stirrup pump? It was as much use as a chocolate kettle. Dat cheap lard dey use went up like gunpowder. Dere was bits of auld cod and mushy peas shot two hundred feet into de air. Begob, I don't know what de world's comin' to at all. Last war it was Belgian nuns, dis war it's chip shops – and to think we wanst had a German piano!'

For my first Christmas present I was given a piece of coal.

'It'll stand de choild in good stead,' said my Grandmother. 'He'll never want for someting to keep him warm so long as he's got dis in his pocket.' And she took up her knitting needles

and began knitting dementedly.

'What's that you're knitting?' asked my Mother.

'It's a book.'

'What's it about?'

'I don't know yet. It's wan o' dem class of books dat starts up wid a lot of introduction bits about countryside and de scenery and dat class of ting. It could end up wid de seduction and eventual doin' away wid herself of a poor milkmaid, or den again it could be a book about swine fever in Dorset!' And she took a pinch of snuff from her snuffbox and poked it up the great cavity of her nose, glaring at my Mother as though daring her to contradict her.

Early in the New Year of 1945 my Grandmother invented potato-flavoured ice-cream. 'It'll become de Oirish national dish,' she cried, looking up from the drawing board, 'togedder wid soda-bread, cruibeens and Guinness! Yer French quiseen will be nowhere on de map at all!'

My Grandmother had very bad hearing and had resorted for years to the use of a wind-up hearing aid. To talk to her, you had to crank the handle of the generator that powered the amplifying system she kept in the pocket of her pinny, as they used to call aprons when I was a child.

'Moussolini's been killed with his mistress!' shouted my Mother one day, cranking the handle like a madwoman making a soufflé.

'Begob, dat's terrible! Did it fall on him at all, or did it catch fire when he was smokin' in bed?'

'Not mattress – mistress!' shouted my Mother, her right arm bulging like Popeye's and a distinct smell of ozone permeating the air.

'Begob, a mistress d'ye say? And him livin' in de same country as de Pope!' said my Gran, crossing herself and getting tangled in the wires. 'But dere's never an ill wind somewhere dat doesn't blow somebody some good. Don't hurricanes kill

10

mainly Protestants and pagans? Didn't de earthquake of San Francisco, as well as destroying de laundries of de poor Chineemen, also destroy de bawdy houses where de poor sailormen were banged on de head wid socks full of wet sand and robbed of everything apart from deir undershirts and deir waterproof Bibles? And didn't it drive de women wid red lips and de silk stockins off de streets altogedder?'

'What's this got do with Moussolini?' asked my Mother, as static building up in the generator earthed itself via the dog, singeing half its fur off and giving it a fixed grin, so that for the rest of its natural life it looked like a member of the British aristocracy.

'Well, with de Eyetallyans out of de runnin' it's time for de Oirish to come into deir own. Bejaysus, I can see it now, splashed on hoardin's across the world, "Mother O'Neill's potato-flavoured ice-cream!" Begob, it could corner the world market.'

But before she could patent the idea a knock on the door of our air-raid shelter, one morning just after the Angelus, announced the arrival of three men with violin cases, moustaches, dark suits and fedora hats.

'It's de Palm Court Orchestra,' said my Gran, putting down her knitting.

They opened the violin cases they were carrying, took out Chicago pianos and pointed them at my Grandmother. The leader of the three, who from his sheer physical presence and his habit of picking his teeth with a razor blade, obviously was the leader, stepped forward, his moustache curled upwards in an ugly leer, like a black slug trying to escape up his nostril. As he came towards my Gran he tripped and fell over the dog. Picking himself up he turned on his two accomplices, who were trying to smother sniggers that were building up inside them like boiling cabbage in a pressure cooker. He fixed the men with a glare that pulled the carpet of hysteria from under them and they fell silent. He turned on my Grandmother.

'Eh, Mamma O'Neill, we from da Mafia.'

'Pleased to meet you, Mr Murphy,' said my Grandmother, extending her hand.

'No, we from da Mafia, we come to do a bigga deal with you. You give us da secret plans a da potato-flavoured icea-creama, we no shoota you. You don' give us da plans a da potato-flavoured icea-creama, we givva you da concrete wellies an' you learn a walk on da bottom a da river.'

'Dat, be de powers, sounds clear enough to me,' said my Gran, handing over the formula. 'Begob, I never wanted to be in de big business anyway.'

And that's how, like that car engine that runs on water and the everlasting light bulb, O'Neill's potato-flavoured ice-cream vanished from the world, never to be seen again, its secret formula hidden somewhere in a vault in Bologna.

Not long afterwards my Grandmother, returning from church in the dark after Bendiction, was chased by a man on a bicycle waving a sausage.

'Was it a Raleigh?' asked my Mother.

'How do I know what make of sausage it was?' said my Gran, furiously knitting me *Noddy joins Sinn Fein*.

'Are you sure it was a sausage?'

'Begob woman, I've had eleven children, thirteen of them livin', de ye think I don't know de difference between a sausage and a bicycle pump?'

Later that year Hitler committed suicide in the bunker, and my Grandmother heard the news as she was knitting another book. She was tired of knitting the classics, which she complained made her arms ache. 'Dem long sentences in dem books be Jane Austen! Begob, dey have me fingers knotted up with de cramp.'

She'd switched recently to knitting true romances with heroes called Trevor and heroines called Celia, who met on country estates or islands in the sun and pursued and counter-pursued each other through 180 pages and twenty-seven balls of three-ply wool. 'Begob, I could knit dem in me sleep. I only ever dropped de stitches de wanst, when a villain called Clark Haggart in a book I was knitting called *The Secret of Castle Greymayne* was about to force his attentions, de blackguard, on Viola, de poor governess to his children who was really de orphan of de Ambassador to Siam, a kindly man with an eye-patch who was killed in a car crash when de Bentley ran off an Alpine road in de snowstorm.'

'What happened?' asked my Mother.

'I knitted de wrong ending,' said my Gran, 'and he had his way wid her in de linen cupboard on page 179.'

'Hitler's dead,' said my Mother, changing the subject.

'Aragh, yer man Hitler's too clever for dat class of yoke altogedder. He'll've shaved de moustache off and escaped disguised as de piano tuner. Him and dat Eva Spam.'

'Braun,' said my Mother.

'I knew it was someting to do wid meat,' said my Gran.

After that, my Gran spent hours of every day wandering the streets, hanging round outside the homes of music teachers, jumping out on piano tuners as they came out of the door, accusing them of being Adolf Hitler. On eleven separate occasions, the police brought her home with tuning-fork marks on the side of her head. On the twelfth occasion my Grandmother was bound over to keep the peace.

'De Germans started it!' she told the magistrate as she was carried from the Court.

On May 8th VE Day was declared. My Grandmother, suspicious as ever, refused to dismantle the blackout blinds. 'Yez can't trust dem Germans,' she muttered. 'It's probably a trick. Dey're only resting for de summer.'

Just in case, however, she took all my sweet coupons out of the coupon book and blew them all on a crate of Guinness from the Dog and Glockenspiel public house at the corner of our street. Four days after everybody else had had their party, she had a party on her own. A bunting-strewn table laden with dried egg and cress sandwiches and a crate of empty Guinness bottles was found blocking the route of the number 81 trolleybus. Underneath it lay my Gran, drunk as several lords, shouting, 'Put that light out!' and, 'Parnell you should never have gone to Brighton!'

When the trolleybus driver approached her under the table she accused him of being a piano tuner, snatched the trolleybus pole out of his hand and smashed the pork butcher's window with it, lassooing a passing window cleaner with a yard of

Cumberland sausage.

'Come out of there!' he shouted at her.

'Get away widyez,' she screeched back. 'Ye've got a face like a turd wid a cap on!'

Our parish priest, Monsignor McGuinness, was called out to calm her down. When he arrived on the scene my Grandmother was nowhere in sight.

'Where is the old fool?' he asked the trolleybus driver, being no stranger to my Gran's peccadillos.

'She's crawled under the trolleybus and is refusing to come out,' said the driver.

The Monsignor got down on his hands and knees and peered into the gloom under the wheels of the bus.

'Who is it?' shouted my Grandmother.

'Monsignor McGuinness,' he shouted.

'Guinness? Of course I do,' she shouted back. 'Can a duck swim?'

The Monsignor, who thought she'd been run over by the trolleybus shouted back, 'Last Rites?'

My Grandmother, deaf as ever replied, 'Of course it's right, it's de only stuff I drink. It keeps me bowels open. Shove us a bottle under.' And she began singing 'Kelly the Boy from Killarney' and 'The Boys from Wexford' as the passengers on the trolleybus muttered and glanced at their watches.

After that, my Grandmother was banned from the church of St Hernia's in Crumpsall from Confession for six weeks and Communion for seven, to run concurrently. In return, indignant as ever, she accused Monsignor McGuinness of being a piano tuner. The Monsignor replied that she was mad and that he'd once played hurley for Ireland.

'So did my cousin Paddy O'Dea, him who died in the treacle flood in Ballysodare, and he didn't go round frightening old ladies under trolleybuses!'

On VJ Day my Grandmother stopped sticking pins in the picture of Emperor Hirohito.

'I knew it'd work,' she said.

'It was the atom bomb,' said my Mother.

'Show me de bomb dat hasn't got atoms in it, and I'll show you a duck widdout a quack!' she said cleverly, ramming a fistful of snuff up her nose.

'Einstein and Oppenheimer,' shouted Aunty Julia, who'd just come in from shaving the gooseberries.

'Who?' asked my Gran.

'Einstein and Oppenheimer!' whispered Aunty Julia, who'd been blinded by the fog of snuff.

'Your Grandfather never bought his suits anywhere else. Dey were de only tailors able to accommodate de special trouble he had after de saddle came off his bike when he was cycling down de church steps in de rain after Midnight Mass.'

16

Aunty Julia was unable to speak for sneezing.

Four days after VJ Day my Grandmother had another street party on her own. This time Monsignor McGuinness refused to go out. 'The woman's a madman,' he said and went back to darning the mouseholes in his chasuble.

Molly, his housekeeper, who just happened to be a cousin of my Gran's from Connemara, took her a piece of dried soda bread as she lay under the trolleybus again.

'Sure, and the man doesn't mean it,' she said.

'Begob, I'd be a long time dead before I'd worry about a Kerryman in a red cucumber,' she said.

'You mean cumerbund, Mary Ellen,' said Molly.

'Dat's all me´arse and Peggy Martin,' said my Gran. 'Why should I say cummerbund when I don't even know what de wan of dem is?'

'I'm talking about the ting he wears round his middle.'

'Dat's a cucumber,' said my Gran, a mouth full of soda bread, 'and nobody will tell me any different.'

'The woman's a madman,' said Molly.

'Get her out from under my trolleybus,' said the driver. 'If I'm late home again my wife will suspect me of having a fancy woman along the route.'

'That's no way to talk to an Irish housekeeper,' said Molly, hitting him with her reliquary containing the knucklebones of St Impetigo.

Eventually, Molly coaxed my Grandmother out from under the trolleybus and together they came hobbling home to our air-raid shelter for a pot of tea like two jackdaws with their lisle stockings and handbags and their black garb and grey hair. I can still see the scene in my mind's eye after all these years. I was almost a year old at the time and I was sitting in my pram before the fire while my Gran and Molly sat either side of the black-leaded grate discussing the relative merits of various newspapers.

'Now your *Daily Herald,'* said my Gran, 'dere's a fine Socialist newspaper for you. Yez only need a one match to dat and yer fire's blazing away in less than seconds. Yer *Times* now, ever since Attlee got in, Churchill's been telling dem to put somethin' in de stuff dey make de paper from to stop it lightin' easy. Ye'd be half a box of matches gone, yer lungs'd be collapsed from puffin' at the few sparks der'd be burnin' on de edge of de ting and de room'd be full of smoke. 'Tis a capitalist plot to force de proletariat to buy firelighters.'

At that time Molly suspected my Gran of Communist as well as Republican tendencies, she herself being more of a pragmatist than anything else, never going anywhere without her rosary beads and her long pink knickers held up with braces and a belt. From her position as the Monsignor's housekeeper she looked down her nose at my Gran and said, a little huffily, 'Mind you, yer *Times* now is a better class of newspaper altogether for cuttin' into squares and hangin' on de nail inside de toilet.'

'Aragh, ye have de point dere,' said my Gran, 'but if ye wants my opinion de best of all fer dat class of yoke is yer *Daily Mirror.'*

'Do ye tell me dat now?' asked Molly, her toothless mouth as round and wrinkled as a semi-deflated swimming ring.

'Aragh I do surely,' said my Gran. 'Yer *Daily Mirror* now has shorter sentences and shorter articles so ye've more chance of gettin' a full article on a backside-sized piece of paper wid de *Daily Mirror* dan ye have wid de *Times* and de *Telegraph* and dat other class of paper. And to add to dat, yer man at de *Times* uses a class of ink dat won't dry properly, so if yez was to be knocked down be a trolleybus de doctor in hospital would tink ye's had been sitting in de coalhole.

'Mother of God, Mary Ellen! Are you tellin' me dat?' said

18

Molly, crossing herself.

'I am surely, and if you want my opinion de only paper for a Catlick backside is de *Daily Mirror*.'

'What about the *Universe?*' asked the innocent Molly.

'God save us, de woman's talking sacrilege!' said my Gran, crossing herself. 'De *Universe* is it? Would yez come on outa dat! Yer might find yerself wiping yer backside wid one of de Holy Ghost Fathers out wid de black babies in Africa, or even de Holy Father himself on de balcony in Rome.'

'Sacred Heart of Jaysus!' said Molly, immediately beginning a decade of the rosary. 'De Monsignor's used nothing but de *Universe* since I ran out of de *Times* last year.'

'De poor man's probably excommunicated himself and doesn't know it,' cackled my Gran, reaching in the fire for the red hot poker she used to mull her Guinness with.

One evening as we sat as usual in the air-raid shelter, my Gran – who'd been to the local cinema to see *Bernadette of Lourdes Meets King Kong* or some such thing – fell through the door scandalised. The Pathé News had shown a new dance called the Bee Bop that the man had said in the commentary was sweeping America.

'Begob, and if it's sweepin' America they're after I don't see what was wrong wid the good Catlick brush! Me brudder Henry Patrick O'Neill went over dere to dig America and he never used anyting, only de shovel. Sweepin' indeed!' she snorted down her nose. 'Divil a bit of sweepin' dey was doin' at all, dey was leppin' about like monkeys.'

'Orang-utans?' said my Mother.

'Dey shot yer Grandfather's brother Finbar in de foot because he wouldn't sell dem any petrol. De poor man was a grocer and didn't keep de stuff. Still, I don't tink he should have offered dem lard instead.'

'That was the Black and Tans,' said my Uncle Bernard, who'd just come back from fighting the Japanese.

'Black! Orange! What does it matter what colour dey were if you've been shot in de foot be dem?' muttered my Gran.

For ever after that she was convinced that Bee Bop was the anti-Christ, and if anything faster than a foxtrot came on the wireless she would hit it with the rosary beads until it turned over from Henry Hall to Hilversum or Droitwich.

Just before Christmas, my Uncle Harry came home from fighting the Germans.

'Your dinner's burnt,' said my Gran. 'Everybody else was home months ago.'

'I missed the bus,' said my Uncle Harry, and my Gran hit him with her rosary beads. 'It's dark in here,' said Uncle Harry, picking himself up off the floor.

'She won't take the blackout curtains down,' said my Mother.

On Christmas Eve a man came round to tune the piano. He had red hair and freckles, a wooden leg, a stammer, one arm, a patch over one eye, no teeth, one ear missing and terminal dandruff.

'You are Adolf Hitler!' said my Gran, threatening him with a freshly-knitted book.

'I wu-wish I wu-was, missus, I wu-wish to GGG-God I wu-was,' he replied nodding fervently, a cloud of dandruff filling the shelter.

We were sitting one afternoon with the radio on listening to Workers' Playtime when the announcer told the waiting world that a man called Churchill was about to speak. My Gran threw a bottle of holy water over the radio. 'Begob, if

20

he's goin' to start another war I'm having nothin' to do wid it.'

But the voice on the radio, the voice of somebody who didn't really believe what he was saying but liked the sound of it, droned on and on about something called the Iron Curtain.

'Begob, more expense,' said my Gran. 'Dey melted down de cemetery railings for gun barrels, now dey'll be coming round for de cellar lids to make dis iron curtain ting wid.'

Then Uncle Harry, who was used to the sun of Africa and could stand the gloom no longer, got up and took down the blackout curtains. For the first time since 1939 sunlight flooded the air-raid shelter, the spiders came out with their hands up, the cat went under the canoe and everybody stared in amazement at a little man with a toothbrush moustache and hair combed to one side crouched in a hitherto dark corner of the room behind the canoe wearing the uniform of the Afrika

Corps and carrying a paintbrush and bucket of whitewash.

'Love of God, who's dat over dere?' cried my Gran.

'Ich bin Adolf Hitler,' said the man, pulling himself up to his full height of four feet three.

'Away wid yer blether, you're a piano tuner!' said my Gran, driving him out of the house with her flailing rosary. 'And don't come frightenin' a good Catlick woman wid yer bicycle and yer sausage again!'

'Was that the man?' asked my Mother.

'Not at all, but he'll do to be goin' on wid,' said my Gran.

2
Two Rabbis In The Tunnel Of Love

I suppose at this point I ought to explain about the canoe, previously mentioned in context with the little man with the toothbrush moustache crouched in the corner of the air-raid shelter.

My Grandmother was a prudent woman in spite of her leanings towards Communism and Republicanism and one afternoon, while she was reading an old copy of *Old Moore's Almanac,* trying to see whether the predictions had come true, she had come across the words 'History repeats itself'.

'Begob, and dat's true for you,' she said. 'Didn't de baker's son in Lisdoonvarna, Sean Dwyer, fall off his bicycle tree times in one month at de same crossroads shouting after Mat de grocer's daughter, Bridget. Dere's history repeatin' itself if ever I saw it.'

Fortified by this evidence of her own concerning the tendency for historical events to duplicate themselves, she became convinced that Noah's Flood would come round again and bought an Indian canoe from a cousin of hers from Clare, Liam Og Na Corcoran who was the boathouse keeper on the boating lake of Bellevue Pleasure Gardens.

'It was rammed only de once,' said Liam Og, 'be de pleasure cruiser *Star of de Lake*. But de cruiser was full of nuns of de order of de Little Sisters of de Poor and it was only goin' slowly on account of de sisters' bad nerves so no harm was done beyond a small hole near de eagle's eye, caused be a lame nun's walkin' stick. It was bein' paddled at de moment of collision by a couple who'd spent too much time in de Tunnel of Love and who'd been dazzled on comin' out into de light.'

'I suppose dey was Protestants?'

'Not at all, dey was a couple of rabbis as respectable as you please, and had only got into de Tunnel of Love in desperation when dey were tryin' to avoid one of de swans which was attackin' dem at de time.'

'And why would a swan attack a rabbi?' asked my Gran, puzzled. 'Was it anti-semitic at all?'

'Get away wid yer bodder,' said her cousin the boatman. 'Yer man de swan would attack anybody wid a beard and a hat on.'

'Were you not after warnin' such a class of gentleman dat the swan was possessive of a tendency to do dis class of yoke?'

'I did surely, and dey took deir hats off and stowed dem in de beak of de canoe.'

'Den in God's name, why did de swan attack dem?'

'Because dey had on, underneath deir hats, dem little skull-cap tings dat betoken hats in de Jewish religion.'

'And de swan attacked dem for dat?'

'De swan knew its Hebraic law and a hat is a hat even when it's a skull-cap,' said my Grandmother's cousin nodding, sagely.

'Begob, it's an intelligent class of swan yez have at the Bellevue Lake.'

'Aragh, yer swan's all right on Hebraic law, but you try him on de geometry and ye'll find as dull a duck as ever dived for chickweed. Yer goose is yer man for geometry and yer calculus.'

'What about de mallard?' asked my Gran.

'Astro-physics and tram timetables of Liverpool 1926 to 1928,' said the boatman. 'When it comes to yer astro-physics and tram timetables of Liverpool 1926 to 1928 yer mallard is de bees' knees.'

So my Grandmother bought the canoe for £4.10s and stocked it with pemmican, peat, soda bread, tea, condensed milk and a year's back copies of the *Universe* to read until the waters subsided.

'There's no room for the animals, Mother,' expostulated my Mother.

'Bugger de animals!' said my Gran. 'Would dey save me if I was drowning? Don't scorpions bite? Would yez put a snake down yer vest? Didn't de swan try and kill de rabbis? De only animal dat's coming wid me and the choild' (and she nodded in my direction) 'is de cat.'

'We haven't got a cat,' said my Mother.

'Exactly,' said my Gran, and she snorted heavily down her nose as she sat knitting *War and Peace*. 'Begob, dese Russian books take some work, I'm tellin' yez. De trouble is once ye've started dem ye can't put dem down.'

1947 was without doubt a traumatic year in my life. I could now walk quite strongly and was allowed, when released from my high chair, to wander freely round the air-raid shelter. I performed a daily circuit from the canoe to the hurdy-gurdy, from there to the dugong's cage and from the dugong's cage to the hearing-aid generator before returning to my chair.

'Begob, he's a great choild for de walking,' said my Gran. 'If he keeps it up like dis we may let him out of de house for a while.'

'He's too young,' said my Mother, 'and beside the sunlight might fade him. You know what happened to the curtains.'

'Don't move the tablecloth,' said my Uncle Bernard, 'I haven't finished reading it. Look what it says here,' and he read, '"Bell Laboratories of America have just invented the transistor."'

'Transistor,' said my Gran, 'do ye tell me dat, now? Begob, before ye know it, it'll be de micro-chip next and God knows it's little enough ye get now for your fourpence wid de fish. Transistors!' and she snorted. 'If God had meant us to have transistors we'd have been born wid printed circuits!'

'It'll make life easier so,' said my Uncle Bernard.

'Begob, and when was life ever easy?' said my Gran. 'Can yer transistor scrub yer steps or peel yer onions? Will yer transistor mend yer motor car when it breaks down?'

'We haven't got a motor car,' said my Mother.

'Begob, and we haven't,' said my Gran. 'And dat's another ting! All dis talk of transistors and me still havin' to walk to Confession! At my age! Half the night on me knees wid de penance dat auld divil McGuinness gives me and me still having half a mile to walk home. Mind youse, de penances nowadays aren't a patch on de penances you'd be gettin' in de auld days. Four Hail Mary's and six Glory Be's for impure thoughts! Begob, you'd get that for answering back to yer Mother in de auld days.'

'Why don't you get a bike?' asked my Uncle Harry, innocently.

'A bicycle, will ye have me ridin' on a bicycle to church? You don't get de class of bicycle here dat you do in Oireland at all. A Catlick woman couldn't be seen dead ridin' a British

27

bicycle. Dere's not enough mudguard to stop de updraught driving de skirt above calf height and showin' yer knees to de world, de handlebars are so low dat yer stoop down exposing de lower troat and de upper chest and what's more, de saddle is too narrow for decency.'

'D'ye tell me dat?' said Molly, who was in the corner sandpapering the dog prior to painting.

'I do,' said my Gran.

'But Mary Ellen, de bicycles we rode in Oireland as girls were all British bicycles and were approved be de Mother Superiors of every convent in Ireland.'

'D'ye tell me dat?' said my Gran.

'I do,' said Molly. 'Don't I remember my own bicycle frame and a little sticker on de down tube saying "approved by the Reverend Mothers of every Convent in Oireland."'

'And so dey were,' said my Grandmother. 'Those bicycles was Oirishised.'

'D'ye tell me dat now?' said Molly.

'I do surely,' said my Gran. 'Every woman's bicycle dat entered Dublin trew the quays or the North Wall, save dose intended for common streetwalkers and circus women, had deir mudguards extended, taller handlebars affixed and a seat widened by de implantation of gutta percha and goose fedders until it was of dimensions approved by de Holy See of Rome.'

'Well now, ye learn somethin' every day,' said Molly, shaving the dog's chin. 'And could you not be gettin' an Oirish bicycle imported from Dublin be yer cousin who works on the Liverpool Docks?'

'I could do and to be sure,' said my Gran, pumping up the blow lamp to tune her xylophone, 'but I wouldn't ride an Oirish bicycle trew de pagan streets of England.'

'And why not?' asked Molly.

'Because de buggers don't go fast enough,' said my Gran.

It was in this year that Al Capone died.

'Hide de violin case, Eileen,' cried my Gran. 'We don't want to be insinuated.'

'Incriminated,' said my Mother.

'D'ye tell me dat?' said my Gran. 'I thought they'd have buried him. Aren't all yer Eyetallyans Catlicks? He must be a Mason – they're the great boys for de incineration.'

'It says in the tablecloth that Henry Ford has just died and left 625 million dollars,' said my Uncle Bernard.

'D'ye tell me dat now,' said my Gran. 'Ford now, dat's an Oirish name. I had a tird cousin on my mother's side called Ford. Fetch me a pen and a bottle of ink, ye never know, we could be heirs to a fortune. I could buy a new walkin' stick.'

'But you don't use a walking stick,' said my Mother.

'God knows I don't,' said my Gran, 'and don't I tank God every day on my knees dat I don't? But yer walkin' stick is a

handier class of ting for killin' burglars wid dan an umbrella. Dere was a time when yer umbrella spines was made wid a good class of Sheffield steel and for 1s 6d yez could buy an umbrella that ye could knock seven policemen over wid. But now, begob, they're using dat imported rubbish from Hong Kong and ye bend de thing wavin' it at cabmen. For tirty-five years I've slept wid an umbrella by me bedside waitin' for de burglars to come climbin' over de roof-tops.'

'What in God's name would a burglar be doing coming to this air-raid shelter?' said Uncle Bernard. 'There's nothing to steal.'

'Dey might tink dey're in next door,' said my Gran, tapping the side of her nose wisely.

My Uncle Bernard carried on reading the tablecloth. 'I see they've got an atomic pile at Harwell,' he said.

'And dat's what comes of sittin' on cold steps,' said my Gran. 'Begob, atomic piles! D'ye tell me dat now? Dey must be de terrible, painful tings.'

It was almost exactly at that moment that my Grandfather returned home from the First World War. 'Where've you been for the last thirty-five years?' snorted my Grandmother. 'Yer dinner's burnt.'

'Some of dem Germans was hard to catch,' said my Grandfather, ducking (he was an old hand at dodging the rosary beads). 'I see you still have the canoe,' said my Grandad, cranking the generator.

'It's handy,' said my Grandmother, 'for keeping the antimacassar in, and if I had a hauteboy or a crumhorn I'd keep dat in it too.'

'D'ye tell me dat?' said my Grandad. 'I'll go down de petshop tomorrow and get you a wan.'

And so it was that the dugong in the cage came to be in our already overcrowded air-raid shelter.

'Don't you tink we could go back in de house, Mary Ellen, de war's been over four years?' said my Grandad, getting up from the tin bath he used as a chair.

'I don't trust dem Germans, and besides de rent man tinks we're still at Blackpool.'

My Grandfather shook his head and went off to the pet shop, returning with a sad-faced dugong. 'Dey had no crumhorns or hauteboys but de man in de pet shop said dis was de next best thing. He was going to wrap it up but I told him that he'd no need to since I'd brought de carrier bag with me.'

'Begob, dat ting's nearly six foot tall,' said my Gran.

'I must admit I experienced some difficulty,' said my Grandfather. 'On de way back home on de bus it started singing "De Ball of Kerrymuir", so I had to put de bag over its head.'

'D'ye tell me dat now?' said my Gran. 'And what would dey call dis class of ting at all?'

'Jim.'

'Begob, de man's a fool! I mean what type or specification of a yoke would it be at all?'

'It's a dugong, according to de man in de shop.'

'D'ye tell me dat now? A dugong! And what sort of food does it eat at all?'

'It eats a stone of fish a day.'

'Araagh! And it's well for you dat'll be de fisherman,' said my Gran laughing to herself heartily, stuffing pinches of snuff up her left nostril. 'And does it talk at all?'

'It used to belong to a sailor and be de example on de bus, I'm afraid it only knows seafaring songs of a scurrilous nature.'

As if on cue, the dugong began to sing 'The Good Ship Venus', until silenced by a blow from my Grandmother's rosary beads.

'I'll wash its mouth out wid soap,' said my Grandmother.

'I forgot to tell you, it eats soap as well,' said my Grandfather.

Two more traumatic events in the year of 1947 were the assassination of Mahatma Gandhi and the nationalisation of the railways. On hearing of the first, as Uncle Bernard sat reading the tablecloth in the air-raid shelter, my Gran immediately ran down to the Police Station to establish an alibi.

'Begob, I never left de country, sor. I was all times in de air-raid shelter feeding de dugong.'

'The dugong?' said the desk-sergeant, putting down his bacon sandwich, sensing either that he was about to uncover an international conspiracy involving Communist revolutionaries or that he was dealing with a madwoman.

'Sure, and we keep de dugong across from de canoe wid de eagle's head dat was damaged be de lame nun's walkin' stick when de two rabbis escaped from de swan in de Tunnel of Love.'

It was at this moment that the desk-sergeant's brain exploded. There was a dull 'thung' sound, and his eyes glazed over just before he hit the floor – stone dead. My Grandmother banged the bell, demanding more attention. The Inspector came out and in the verbal scuffle that followed she was arrested for using surrealist explanations with intent to wound or cause a disturbance of the peace. She was taken to the Magistrates' Court where, for the second time in three years, she was bound over to keep the peace.

'De Germans started it!' she shouted, as she was led from the Court.

When the railways were nationalised Monsignor McGuinness declared from the pulpit of St Hernia's, Crumpsall, that the Labour Party was the anti-Christ.

'Aragh! Yer man McGuinness was only a grocer's son from Kilorglin,' said my Grandmother. 'His father never wore a proper pair of trousers in his life, only pairs his wife, de mad Reilly's daughter, made from cut-down sugar bags so dat he was known throughout Kilorglin as "Tate and Lyle McGuinness".'

'D'ye tell me dat?' said Molly.

'I do indeed,' said my Gran. 'In fact, me cousin Jim Lynot told me dere was even a song about him made up be Willy Crowley, de Cork Balladeer, called "De Ballad of Tate and Lyle McGuinness".'

'D'ye tell me dat?' says Molly.

'I do surely,' said my Gran, and she launched into song with a voice that sounded like someone tipping coke down a corrugated iron roof. To the tune of 'The Garden Where the Praties Grow' she sang:

Well, if you'll gadder round me den a story I will tell,
Of de grocer Mat McGuinness, I swear I knew him well.
He never wore de breeches to keep out de wintry air,
But his wife cut down de sugar bags to make himself a pair.

Oh ladle-ee id'll deedle id'll diddly id'll dooo!

Well de boys all shouted 'sugar lumps!' as he went down the street,
And de tinkers shouted 'Tate and Lyle' and 'Barney, where's yer feet?'
But de Grocer never minded dem, he slung dem a deaf ear
Sayin' 'Begod, dese home-made trousers save me pounds and pounds a year.'

Oh ladle-ee id'll deedle id'll diddly id'll dooo!

When his Grandmother she got married the whole of Kerry came,
To see if Tate and Lyle would wear some trousers or be shamed,
But Begod, de devil a pair he wore but a brand new pair of sacks,
Wid 'Handle wid Care' across de front and 'Use no hooks' across de back.

Oh, ladle-ee id'll deedle id'll diddly id'll dooo!

'Wan singer, wan song,' said Molly, banging the table. 'Up de yard dere's a hum of hay of yez and we'll have two more bottles of Guinness in de snug.'

It was round about this time, too, that my Grandmother began to imagine that the window cleaner was a Russian spy. How it happened was like this. It was one morning three or four days before Christmas, when my Uncle Bernard, who was on his knees reading the firelighters, announced in a trembling voice,

34

'The Russians have exploded the atomic bomb!'

'D'ye tell me dat now?' said my Gran, who was furiously knitting *Under Milkwood*. 'In dat case I'm not leaving dis air-raid shelter till I hear de all-clear. Harry, fetch me de stirrup pump and me air-raid warden's hat. Are you sure it's de Russians and not yer Germans coming back?'

'It says here that the Russians have exploded the atomic bomb,' said my Uncle Bernard, 'and the firelighter never lies.'

'And where would yer Russians get such a class of formula to make a yoke like dat?' asked my Gran.

'It seems there's some spies selling secrets of the building of the atomic bomb to the Russians.'

'It's de window cleaner,' said my Gran firmly, her mouth closing as tightly as a goldfish's bum. 'He's an atheist so it must be him.'

'How in God's name do you work that out?' asked my Mother.

'All Communists are atheists, all Russians are Communists, therefore all atheists are Russians.'

'But what about the Catholics in Russia?' asked my Mother. 'The *Universe* says there's millions of them.'

'Dey're all Oirish,' said my Gran. 'Dey're de Wild Geese dat went to fight wid Napoleon and when dey realised dat he had piles and heartburn, being true-born Oirishmen dey refused to follow him any more and got jobs on de building sites of Moscow. Begob, wasn't it de Countess Markievicz herself dat was running guns into Oireland for de Easter Rising? Dere's proof if yez ever needed it dat some Russians are Oirishmen and some Oirishmen are Russian.'

'Did Napoleon have piles and heartburn?' I asked. It being the first time I have spoken in this book.

'Begob, and he did, choild. De yez tink a man widdout piles would walk back from Moscow and it being full of horses, on account of de demise of great numbers of de French cavalry in de cold, dem havin' no vests? If yer man Napoleon hadn't had de piles he'd've been lepping on de back of one of dem horses and been away like Murphy's dog before you could say Christopher Robinson. And when it comes to de heartburn did yez ever see a picture of Napoleon widdout ye'd see him wid de one hand inside his gansey. That's a sure sign of yer heartburn!' And she snorted down her nose.

'Aragh, yer heartburn is yer powerful class of ailment,' said Molly. 'I had it so bad de wanst I bit de knob off de cupboard door and couldn't get it open for a year.'

'It wasn't the heartburn at all,' said my Uncle Bernard, 'he was looking for his wallet.'

'Would yez come on outa dat!' said my Gran. 'Yer man had no need of money at all wid ev'ry corporal, quartermaster and drummer boy in de French army struggling to buy him drinks. Yer man never bought a drink in his life.'

'D'ye tell me dat?' said Molly. 'And wasn't dey after naming a brandy after him?'

'And why not?' shouted my Gran. 'What else would you call it? Jim? Sean? Percy? Would yez buy a brandy called Eric?'

Molly thought for a moment.

'Yez have me dere, Mary Ellen, and I don't suppose soldiers would have followed a man called Eric Bonaparte to de gates of Moscow either.'

'And yez can be sure dey wouldn't,' laughed my Gran, her false teeth rattling together like marbles falling down stairs.

Convinced that the window cleaner was a Russian spy, my Grandmother began laying traps for him, following him on his rounds and dogging his every footstep until one day the window cleaner, who could take it no more, turned round and screamed in a loud voice, 'Missis! Bog off!'

My Grandmother came home that night in triumph. 'Begob, I have de proof positive now dat he's de Russian spy. Didn't he have to turn round and call me a Russian name dis mornin'?'

'D'ye tell me dat?' said Molly.

'I do surely, he thought I was some class of woman called Mrs Bogoff.'

Two days later she saw him climbing through the window of number 17 Sebastopol Terrace where the window cleaner – unknown to my Grandmother – was having an affair with the woman of the house, Mrs Violet Blott. This Mata Hari of Sebastopol Terrace was married to an ex-wrestler and professional tram-shunter, who stopped trams with his head and towed them with his teeth, called Jim Blott. My Grandmother took the ladders down from under the window and, phoning the tram depot, told Mr Blott that a Russian spy was in the house with his wife. Mr Blott arrived home unannounced; the window cleaner, discovering himself with no visible means of escape, jumped from the window and landed on a passing lorry, concussing himself. The lorry was taking a consignment of rocking horses and cream crackers via Archangel and the Manchester Docks to Irkutz and the headlines in the *Manchester Evening News* the next day read 'Crumpsall Window Cleaner Discovered Unconscious on Russian Ship'.

'Dat only goes to show,' said my Grndmother, 'yer window cleaner now is a foxy class of tradesperson. Dat'll be caused be all dis lookin' in through de people's windows to see what class of furniture would be inside.'

One morning my Grandfather, who had taken up an interest in astronomy after discovering a copy of Professor Pandolfo's *Guide to the Firmament,* came in and announced to the entire family, 'Yer man, now, Columbus was an eejit.'

'And how do ye come to dat conclusion now?' asked my Gran.

'I've been making de calculations and I've reached de conclusion dat yer man Columbus was in de pay of de Masons.'

'D'ye tell me dat now?' said Molly.

'I have de calculations made, and if yez look at dis ye'll see dat de sun at its closest to de Earth is x million miles away.' And he drew on a piece of paper a sausage shape like so:

and traced a line around it so

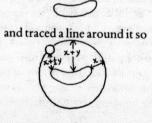

'When it's furthest away from de Earth it's x+y million miles away, and when it's in de middle it's x+½y million miles away. De sun travels round de Earth wonst a day and it takes a year to get from x to y and back again. Darefore de world is not circular at all, because if it was then x would be de same all de time. Darefore de world is shaped like a sausage or a banana. De Equator' (and he drew a banana shape in the dust) 'runs round de skin so' (and he drew a line circling the banana) 'and de sun goes round in a circle. Darefore at some times de sun is further away from de Earth than it is at others.'

'But Grandad, the Earth goes round the sun,' I said.

'Not at all! If de Earth was going round we'd all be dizzy and fall over.'

'But what makes night and day?' I asked.

'Dat's on account of de turning up or down of de current in de sun.'

'But I was reading in a book that it's hotter in some parts of the world than it is in others,' I told him.

'Dat's so de poor Africans in de Congo – who have no clothes at all, never mind de benefit of Holy Mother Church – don't freeze to death. For de same reason yer Eskimos on de North Pole have a mighty superabundance of furs, so yer Arctic is just de place for dem.'

'Mother of God, isn't yer education a great ting,' said my Grandmother, blessing herself. As if to confirm that education was indeed a great thing, the very next day I left the comfort of our air-raid shelter and was enrolled in an educational Colditz that went by the pseudonym of school.

3

You Can See The Angel's Bum, Miss Worswick!

The school I was sent to – which, to protect the innocent, I'll call St Hernia's primary mixed Catholic infants – was in a converted disused abattoir on the north side of the city. The headmaster was an ex-submariner with one leg and a curly ginger wig called Jim Flint. His name was Mr Parker and why he called his wig Jim Flint I'll never understand. Parker, or Nosey as we used to call him, would fall asleep during any sentence lasting more than four words – whether he was speaking them or listening to them. He had as little as possible to do with affairs in the school, preferring instead to stay alone in his room playing the triangle (on which he was a virtuoso) and working on a major novel he was writing, set in the Isle of Man. Like every other novel before or since set in the Isle of Man it was doomed to remain unpublished. After all, who really wants to hear about an unsuccessful love affair between a steward of the Isle of Man Steam Packet Company and a Douglas deck chair attendant?

On my first day at school I was taken by my Mother to the school gates and, when she found they were locked, she threw me over the wall. 'And don't come back till you've learnt something!' she shouted.

As I picked myself up from the playground floor I noticed a small figure in baggy trousers eyeing me speculatively. 'Do you want to buy any fags?' he asked, puffing on a flying cloud.

I shook my head.

'A woman?' was his next suggestion. 'A bottle of pale ale? Dirty postcards? Some black market jelly babies?'

'Whose class are you in?' I asked.

'I'm a teacher,' he snarled, his boot proving the old adage that leather is harder than the skin of your backside.

My class teacher, Miss Worswick, was a nice old lady who on my first day in her class showed me how to roll a plasticine snake. I knew that school was going to be an unlucky place for me when the snake bit me. A swarthy-looking boy sitting at my side saw me crying and offered me his hankie. I ate it.

Later, in the playground, the school bully Fats Molloy swaggered over towards me. 'You're a new kid, aren't you?' he sneered, giving my ear a vicious tweak with a pair of pliers.

'Yes,' I answered, my voice a half-whisper.

'The new kid's going to blub,' he laughed out loud to the ring of cronies standing about him.

'No I'm not,' I shouted, 'I don't blub.' And I drew my fist back and threw a right hook that connected fair and square with the bike shed wall. Then the sky fell on my head, stars exploded in my brain and I woke up on the floor beside my bed.

'I had a bad dream,' I told my Mother as she picked me up.

'No, you didn't. Fats Molloy beat the crap out of you and tomorrow you're going to get your own back.'

'You mean you're going to teach me to box?'

'No, your Grandmother's going to lend you her gun.'

The next morning, after assembly, I passed word along the lines waiting to go into class that I wanted to see Molloy at playtime and I was going to beat him into jam. That morning was the longest morning of my life. As the playtime bell rang I picked up my violin case and left the room.

'Where are you going with that, Harding?' asked Miss Worswick, chewing her cigar.

'I'm just going to play a few tunes, Miss Worswick.'

'Well, don't get blood on my bike.' She winked broadly, her nose and glasses falling on the desk lid as she did so.

At the bike shed a large crowd had gathered. Bernadette McClusky, who would show you her knickers for a jelly baby, was on the edge of the crowd looking towards me. Our eyes met. I saw something there deeper than jelly baby addiction – it was either love or indigestion. I was only five years old, I didn't know the difference. (To be honest, I still don't.)

The crowd cleared as I approached. The chants of 'made you look, made you stare, made the barber cut your hair' died as I approached.

Some girls on the edge of the crowd, skipping to the sing-song cry of 'salt, mustard, vinegar, pepper', mustarded when they should have peppered and fell down in a tangled heap showing next week's washing. All those jelly babies I'd saved. But today my mind was on other things. I pushed my way through the crowd. Molloy was smoking a toffee cigarette, casually sitting on the saddle of a Raleigh Rudge, toffee smoke coming out of his mouth in rings. He'd invented the Polo. Half-hidden in his sock, but plain enough to see by its handle sticking out above the elastic top, was a rubber dagger. If he wanted to play dirty he was going to get it dirty. He saw me coming. His eyes narrowed. Then he saw the violin case.

'Hey,' he called, open-eyed, 'the new kid's going to play the violin!'

'That's right,' I quipped, bending down and undoing the latches of the violin case.

Inside, glistening, sleek and shiny in the morning sun, was a .35 violin. It's hard when even your own grandmother does the dirty on you. I took it out of its case.

'What would you like?' I asked Molloy.

'Do you know I would like to shove that violin up your bum!'

I only knew the first few bars so I started by playing those and then segued into 'The Big Rock Candy Mountain.'

I woke up on the bedroom floor. The violin marks on my head told me it wasn't a dream.

'D'you tell me dat now?' said my Gran when I told her. 'Your poor Grandfather shot Monsignor McGuinness in de leg last night while playing wid de parish ceilidh band. He

tried to play "The Gander in the Pratie Hole" on a Thompson machine gun and peppered a prelate instead. Begob, dere was hell and a half to play. His case comes up next week.'

I knew that if life at school was going to be worth living I had to settle Molloy once and for all. I had been reading a book called *Jungle Jim – Failed Accountant* about an accountant who fails his final accountancy exams and goes to Africa to become a wild animal trapper. I wondered if some of his methods could be of service in the case of Harding versus Molloy. A pit trap was out of the question – the playground was too hard for me to dig one. Poison arrows were hard to get hold of and I was too young to get a licence for an elephant gun. There was one story that gave me an idea: Jim – trapped in a jungle clearing, his leg half torn off, his double-entry ledger lying useless on the floor – is about to become elevenses for a non-vegetarian lion. But as the lion leaps, Jim remembers a trick taught him by an old Yoruba tribesman and begins singing 'Stormy Weather', 'The Soldiers of the Queen', and 'A Little of What You Fancy Does You Good'. The lion stops in its tracks and, convinced that it is seeing things (a singing dinner? It must be that bit of over-ripe wildebeest I ate), staggers off looking for an Alka-Seltzer.

At playtime the next day Molloy came towards me as I stood learning to skip with Philomena O'Grady. 'Hey, new kid.'

I looked – his eyes were mean, half-crazed. Spittle flecked the corners of his mouth; there was sherbet dust on his chin and down the front of his pullover. So that was it! He was on drugs!

'Yes,' I croaked through lips that felt like dried wash leathers.

He came towards me – a fist like five pounds of Cumberland

sausages was raised aggressively towards my face.

I began singing 'On The Good Ship *Lollipop*' in a high childish voice, but by the time I'd come to the candy shop I'd woken up on the bedroom floor.

My Auntie Jessica, who was a fervent Catholic (even more fervent than the rest of us, and that took some doing) said, 'Be de powers, Michael, you'll have to do what de Lord himself did and turn de other cheek.'

The next day, when he hit me, I turned the other cheek and he hit that one too – proving how stupid God is.

It came to me slowly that there was only one way to beat Molloy. I had to be bigger and stronger than him. To achieve that overnight was impossible, therefore I had to *appear* to be bigger and stronger than him. Next morning before school I took a balloon and painted it black. Then, when it had dried, I painted 'One ton' on it. I had seen Korky the Cat do this in the *Dandy,* so I knew it worked. Then I stuffed rags up my jersey sleeves until I had got muscles like Popeye and put a car inner tube inside my jersey around my chest, pumping it up so that my chest looked huge.

As I waddled through the school playground, a silence descended on the mob. Bernadette McClusky dropped her frock and waved away the queuing jelly baby holders. Molloy was showing off to some of his friends by bending school railings with his teeth. I shouted, 'Hey Molloy,' but the tube was pressing my chest so much it came out as a hoarse whisper.

Molloy, sensing my presence, turned round. I picked up the balloon and held it over my head. The crowd gasped, and whispers of 'One ton' ran through the air. To the admiring glances and open mouths of my fellow infants I held the balloon aloft for almost four minutes. Then, slowly, the balloon began to go down, draping itself round my hand with a slow hissing noise.

Molloy came toward me. His first punch knocked me against the bike shed and a nail sticking out of one of the wooden uprights pierced the inner tube. There was a rushing noise and, with a speed approaching that of light, I shot across the playground straight into Molloy – my head catching him under the chin like a bullet. This time *he* woke up on the bedroom floor, and for the rest of my school career he left me alone.

Our teacher, Miss Worswick, was obsessed by several things: the price of plasticine, whether the school drum, triangle, cymbal, chime bar, pencil on jam jar and kazoo band was going to be up to scratch, and whether the school nativity play was going to be yet another horrific disaster.

'Children,' she shrilled, 'at Christmas time we will have our nativity play and this year it's going to be a success. What is it

47

going to be, Clegg?'

'Do you have to use a pencil, Miss Worswick?'

Clegg was one of those individuals (common to life at large as well as to most infant schools) who, when asked a question – particularly when asked whether they understand something which has just been explained to them – always try and disguise the fact that they have not been listening by asking a question themselves. Such people usually become politicians, policemen or VAT inspectors.

Clegg was the leader of a gang of anti-intellectuals in our school who thought being able to count further than ten was a sign of latent homosexuality. The consequence of this was that anyone who didn't want to get his head kicked in, or at the very least find himself with the label 'sissy' affixed, pretended not to be able to count beyond nine. The result was that most boys in our class were regarded by our teachers as educationally subnormal.

'No, you do not have to use a pencil, Clegg. What do we use pencils for in this school?'

'Sticking in people,' smirked Clegg, he of the ready quip but bad memory forgetting that Miss Worswick could do things with a wooden ruler that would make an SAS man fill his pants. We picked him up off the floor, dusted him and sat him down again, as Miss Worswick went on to explain why this year's nativity was going to be a success.

Apparently, the year before, Miss Worswick had read in *Filmgoer's Companion* that 20th-Century Fox were scouring the streets of England looking for child talent. Determined that none of the brats in her charge should miss a chance of starring in *Frankenstein Meets the Secret Seven*, she wrote to 20th-Century Fox inviting them to the school play – and they accepted. All had gone well until one of the first-year infants (playing St Joseph) piddled on the stage. The two infants playing the donkey had slipped in it, crashing into the

Christmas tree. A Christmas tree light bulb inside a tiny plastic Cinderella's coach had gone into the goldfish bowl, and boiled the goldfish. The wires on the tree's lights had shorted on to the hamster's cage, and the hamster on his treadmill had achieved three thousand revolutions per minute. Just before the fuses of the system had blown, the stick insects had gone up in flames and there was a Kentucky fried budgie on the bottom of the cage. The RSPCA had rushed in with tiny stretchers and carried out the casualties but little could be done. The sight of uniformed men giving the kiss of life to gerbils and stick insects had been so pitiful that one of the talent scouts had had a heart attack and died on the spot.

So this year 'the tinies' – as we first-year infants were known – were reduced from the status of thespians to that of pit orchestra. My Grandmother was very proud. We had recently left the air-raid shelter and moved back into the house (where there was more room for her canoe and her collection of rare bluebottles) so that now, finding her grandson blossoming out into a young Mozart, a mini-Menuhin, a pocket Paderewski, her joy was boundless.

'Be de powers! D'ye tell me dat now?' she cried, puffing out the black bombazine of her chest like a tropical storm cloud. 'And what species of music would youse be playing now? Is it de sympathies you'd be playing or de suets?'

I said it was neither symphony nor suite but the carols for the school Christmas nativity play.

'Begob, and didn't Beethoven start on de comb and paper? Youse all have to start somewhere, as de old lady said when she bit de arse off de sugar elephant. Yer Grandfather's uncle, "Dan de Man", he was yer man for de concertina. Be de powers I'm tellin' yer, he could get a tune out of a brick de way he had de musical fingers, but de concertina, now dat was his forte. Till de bad accident he had, dat is, when he never touched de concertina again.'

49

'What happened?' I asked.

'Well, yer too young to understand completely, but basically it was on account of de concertina havin' bellas and when yer squeeze de concertina de bellas come togedder and one night, at a wake it was – poor Eamonn McBride had been smokin' thick twist in de church paraffin stove and had ended up all over de village. Well, he was at de wake, de crack was mighty and de dancin' was goin' strong when Dympna Crowley, a big strong Connemara girl who was over here workin' on the buildins', backed into de bellas and yer Great-grand-uncle Dan squeezin' dem to get de triplets out in "Merrily Killed de Quaker" nipped her bum wid de bellas!'

'What happened?'

'She did tings to yer Great-grand-uncle Dan and his concertina dat should only go on between a doctor and his patient, and as a result of which he rode a bicycle standin' up for de rest of his days.'

As the days passed and we drew nearer to the date of the nativity play, the school triangle, chime bar, drum, wood block, kazoo and pencil on jam jar band, practised every day with desperate determination. The rhythm section staged a walk-out one day when Miss Worswick told Bernard Rigby he had as much sense of rhythm as a broken rocking-horse. But after a huddled consultation in the stock cupboard, the shop steward of the scissors and gummed-paper table smoothed things over.

We were to perform 'Silent Night', 'We Three Kings', 'While Shepherds Watched', 'Away In a Manger' and 'Gentle Jesus Do Not Stir'. My job was to watch the triangle player next to me and every time he hit his triangle I had to hit my chime bar. I was very nervous. So much so that every time I hear triangles I still get that tingling feeling you get just before you have a pee. I even took my chime bar home to practise.

'Begob, de child's a genius! Would youse listen to him! He has de touch of an angel. Begob he'd bring tears from a glass eye wid his playin'.'

The dugong, unable to stand the noise any more, left home one cold grey November afternoon as the pigeons were lining up outside the PDSA for their cough mixture. 'Tank God for dat,' said my Grandad, tearing up his season ticket to Fleetwood. 'No more bloody fishin'.'

As the day of the performance approached tension within the infants' school heightened, flare-ups were common. There was an incident one day over the sand tray which left three of us with bloodied noses and underpants full of sand. And one afternoon, her nerves shot to pieces with the strain, the lead pencil-on-jam-jar player locked herself in the Wendy house and took an overdose of jelly babies. Miss Worswick made her drink some school milk and she brought the whole lot up in the quiet corner.

The day before the performance we had a dry run that left Miss Worswick grey-faced and determined to leave us all and become a steam-roller driver in the Antarctic. In a daze we wandered home, our sense of reality wiped out, our ears ringing with the sound of chime bars and kazoos, our eyes filled with the shadowy visions of children bent double and joined shoulder to waist being donkeys and asses and Miss Worswick, her ruler flailing like a propeller, trying to turn forty or so infants into a combination of the Hallé Orchestra, the Royal Shakespeare Company and the Moscow Ballet.

P for Performance Day arrived, after a sleepless night spent biting the pillow and imagining the worst – the drum section taking fits, the kazoos filling up with spit as had happened at the rehearsal, my chime bar going out of tune – I staggered bleary-eyed and trembling through the school gates, my Grandmother's holy communion medal hung around my neck. 'Begob it'll bring you luck so,' she had called as I left the house in a daze.

Miss Worswick ushered us all into the hall and, arranging the orchestra on the front benches, gave us all a last briefing. 'Right, children. The orchestra begins with "Silent Night", very quiet and gentle now. Not so hard on the chime bars you boys. You sounded like a fire alarm yesterday. Then the Holy Couple – don't do that Philomena you'll get your fingers stuck – come on from the left with the donkey and the Baby Jesus. They put the baby in the manger and kneel down to adore him with the donkey standing just behind them. Now have you got that?'

'Do we have to use a pencil Miss Wors–' asked Clegg, his last utterance lost in the sound of Education Committee wood on skull. Thinking that was the signal to begin the orchestra began playing, all at different times and speeds, and had to be brought to a standstill with the ruler.

'Now –', said a sweating Miss Worswick, 'after the Holy Family the Three Kings come to the stable to lay their gifts of gold, frankincense and myrrh – and don't drop that tea caddy with the frankincense in, Peter Gittins. That's got to go back to Miss MacWalters after the play.

'Who comes after the Three Kings?

'The answer is not three aces, Terence Tarpey. I'll see you later!

'After the Kings it's the turn of the Shepherds to enter, and the Shepherds lay the little fluffy lamb at the foot of the manger and group themselves with the Three Kings around the Holy Family. Then the Archangels come and bow before the Holy Family and we sing the last hymn "Gentle Jesus Do Not Stir". Have you all got that?'

A tiny voice began 'Do we have to use a pen–' and was

silenced by a glance from Miss Worswick that could have curdled milk.

'Now,' she cried, clapping her hands together so hard that the works flew out of her watch, her voice unnaturally shrill with excitement, 'time for your costumes!'

We watched on, we lowly pit musicians, as the players donned their motley and just as the last child was transformed from a grubby infant with runny nose into a thing of beauty, the parents, grandparents and friends who made up the audience arrived. The first to come in was my Grandmother who, impatient at being kept out of the hall until we were ready by Mr Tierney, the man who taught the big boys, dropped him to the floor with a head butt crying, 'I'm de Grandmother of de lead chime bar player and a member of de Legion of Mary Provisionals! Get out of de way or I'll skelp yez.'

The hall filled up. My Grandmother, Grandfather and Mother were there waving at me frantically – as though killing flies. When all were seated on the benches and the tiny infant chairs Miss Worswick nodded and Mr Walpurgis, the religion teacher, turned off the hall lights. Four bulbs in biscuit tins were hung above the stage, throwing a fitful gloom on to an orange box, marked Outspan, full of straw that was to be a manger. That in its turn stood before a blanket marked War Department Property that was to be seen as the wall of a stable in Bethlehem. A lone star made from milk bottle tops wrapped around pea sticks descended slowly from the ceiling. As the lights dimmed my Grandmother's voice cried out, 'Mother of God, I've gone blind!' but it didn't stop her opening a bottle of Guinness on the back of the seat in front of her.

Someone turned the stage lighting up a little and in the reflected glow I could see the school headmaster, Nosey Parker, already fast asleep. His chin dug into his chest and his top lip was flapping like a draught excluder as he breathed in and out. Beside him sat Monsignor McGuinness, his hands joined together across a red cummerbund that was straining over a belly filled with the potatoes and soda bread with which his housekeeper, Molly, was slowly but surely turning him into a lard mountain. In the corner, at the piano, ready to lead the school orchestra through the minefield of the tonic sol-fa system was Miss MacGoebels: a shadowy figure who had a deep fruity voice tinged with more than a hint of Bavaria, she sported duelling stars and shaved twice a day. The last four rows were composed entirely of patients from the local mental hospital whose treat it was, once a year, to be brought to our school nativity play. Before us was a sea of waiting faces, each and every one transported back to his or her own childhood when the mystery of the tiny room in a backstreet inn in Bethlehem meant more than indigestion, funny hats, and the Queen's speech echoing round plates thick with solidifying gravy after Christmas dinner.

Miss Worswick nodded, and a solo kazoo took up the refrain of that most beautiful of carols, 'Silent Night'. The high notes proved too much for the lead kazoo player's nerves. She dried to drop an octave, misjudged it and burst out crying, the kazoo still in her mouth. The resultant sound was that of somebody kicking to death a large singing bumble bee.

Miss MacGoebels hurriedly brought the rest of the orchestra in with a crashing chord on the piano. I played well, if a little ambitiously, and stretched the tempo too much in the *largo* passage, which brought glares from Michael Coffee on second triangle next to me. We struggled through the number, finally ending on seveal discords, the music collapsing as though somebody had pulled the rug out from underneath it.

The Holy Couple approached from the area reserved for water play. Dressed in a blue tablecloth, impossibly miscast as the Virgin Mary, was Bernadette McClusky, she of the jelly babies, in her arms the bald pot doll from the Wendy house wrapped in a roller-towel swaddling cloth that had 'Manchester Corporation Education Department' printed all the way round it. In our version of the play, the birth in the stable had been dropped as being either suggestive or distasteful – after a student teacher a few years previously had done the whole bit, hot water, screams, the lot, and had had people passing out all over the place.

After Mary came St Joseph, alias Louis Lorenzini, the son of a local ice-cream manufacturer. Louis was really six foot tall, although only six years old. He had been dressed in a brown tablecloth and crêpe-paper beard. His foot had inadvertently been sewn into the hem of his garment so that when he stood up he was bent double in his costume. The crêpe-paper beard had been stuck on with spirit gum which had dried pulling his face out of shape, so that one eye was closed completely while the lower lid of the other was pulled so far down his cheek he looked for all the world as though he had just fallen off the bells of Notre Dame.

At Mary's entrance the hall had whispered universally in admiration, crying, 'Isn't she lovely?' 'You'd wonder how anyone could hurt them, wouldn't you?' and 'Oh! What a bonny little child!'

St Quasimodo's entrance, however, stunned them all into total and absolute silence. There was nothing – just a horrified wordless void, broken by my Grandmother's loud, 'Begob, de poor choild! It's Lourdes he should be going to, not Betlehem.'

There were other murmurs of 'What a shame', and 'You'd think they wouldn't have given him a part, looking like that.'

After the couple had arranged themselves round the orange box, the Ox and the Donkey appeared. They had been got ready by a student teacher who was with us at the time and who was into African art. From cardboard boxes and blankets she constructed things that at rehearsal had frightened one of the dinner ladies into a crying fit so that she had to be led outside blessing herself and asking for a priest.

From halfway down the Donkey as it shuffled along the aisle towards the stage came the cri de coeur, 'Cor, Thingy, your bum doesn't half smell in here!'

Miss Worswick, who had heard this, intercepted the Donkey just as it was passing Monsignor McGuinness and jabbed it with her ruler saying, 'Shut up! Shut up!' From halfway down the Donkey a little voice, tearful but brave, cried, 'But it's true, Miss Worswick! His bum really smells! Really, really. I fink I'm going to be sick!'

Miss Worswick snarled, 'Well if you are – do it quietly!'

The Three Kings and the Shepherds managed to make their way on to the stage without much in the way of mishap, except that one King got the point of his crown entangled with a Shepherd's headdress so that they entered locked together at the head.

'Begob, first it's hunchbacks, now it's Siamese twins,' I could hear my Grandmother mutter.

They assembled on stage behind the Holy Family and the animals, singing 'Away in a Manger' as we valiantly banged and hummed away, Miss MacGoebels leading us like Napoleon retreating from a musical Moscow. As the music grumbled to a tuneless halt a tiny voice on stage cried, 'You know, Thingy, your bum really smells and I'm really really going to be sick.'

Miss Worswick dashed behind the curtains, and lashed out in the general direction of the Donkey, hitting a King instead. The King, thinking he had been nudged by the Ox, hit it. The front end of the Ox kicked a Shepherd, who thumped a King who bit the Donkey who hit another Shepherd so that within seconds the stage was a mêlée of flying fists before which the Virgin Mary and Quasimodo sang in tuneless harmony.

> We will rock you, rock you, rock you,
> We will rock you, rock you, rock you,
> Here's a fur to keep you warm,
> Softly round your tender form.

In the meantime, the last actors in this comedy of errants were getting ready in the stock cupboard. These were the angels who would appear in silent devotion before the saviour, the messiah in his manger in the stable. The plan was that the Archangels would appear on stage with wires affixed to their backs. These went up through the ceiling into the loft on a pulley system, which meant that, after adoring the child in the manger, each of the Archangels could be hoisted heavenwards by three of the strongest boys in the top class, who were backstage hauling hard on the wires. The three angels were got ready by Miss MacWalters, a gentle little lady who could no more say 'goose' to a goose than 'boo'. She lined up the three boys who were about to play a part in the greatest drama ever told. One of them was my friend Wharfie, about whom books could be – and have been – written.

'Now, you boys, I want you to take off all your trousers and put on your angel's costumes,' she said, handing them their white smocks. These had cardboard wings gummed on the back, and a halo, made from a piece of brass wire that came out of the middle of the wings and would hang over their heads for all the world like a mark of holiness. Now my friend Wharfie was a very uncomplicated person. He took whatever was said to him at its literal meaning. Miss MacWalters' words, 'Take off all your trousers' meant nothing less than that to Wharfie. He took off his trousers and his underpants as well as his shoes and socks, putting his smock over the tiny little vest he wore. The smock came to just below the cheeks of his bum. Then, with the other two Archangels, he turned to face the door of the stock cupboard and waited for the cue to enter. We, in the meantime, were watching Miss MacGoebels as she sat at the piano and waiting for her to nod so that we would begin playing 'While Shepherds Watched Their Flocks By Night' – the cue for the three angels to make their way on to the stage. She nodded and, with cables fixed to the harnesses that ran round their waist and shoulders, the three angels one by one came out of the stock cupboard as we began banging and thumping our way through the tune. Slowly they walked, hands together, eyes wide open, the wires of their flying apparatus trailing before them. On to the stage they walked in line, ascending by a tiny wooden staircase that led up to the waiting group in the manger in Bethlehem. There was no room for them to go behind the manger to adore the tiny infant lying there in the straw, symbol of all our hopes and fears, so they stood with their backs to the audience facing upstage. At the words 'The angel of the Lord came down, and glory shone around' all three angels bent to adore the child in the manger.

Michael Coffee, second chime bar player, sat next to me. Suddenly, he threw his chime bar over his head and in a voice which could be heard for streets around, screeched, 'You can see the angel's bum, Miss Worswick!'

There was pandemonium.

Children all over the hall shouted in horror. Miss Worswick, anxious to quell a riot, gave the signal for the angels to ascend into heaven. Heavenwards they went, one of the angels being pulled too enthusiastically hit the ceiling, dislodging a lump of plaster, and snapped his cable so that – without heavenly aid – he descended unangelically on to the piano where he landed with a bang that shut the lid on Miss MacGoebel's fingers.

'Shitezen!' she yelled.

'I'd have said de same myself,' muttered my Gran, 'under de circumstances.'

The big boy in the wings, thinking that Miss MacGoebels had shouted 'Right', banged the gong that was the signal for the school jam jar and pencil, kazoo, triangle, wood block and chime bar band to play the last hymn. Somehow we got it wrong and played 'Silent Night' and 'Away in a Manger' at the same time. One of the patients from the mental hospital got up and started waltzing on her own, and when Monsignor McGuinness stood to make her sit down again she grabbed him and carried on dancing, dragging him round the room, with her arms locked firmly round him. The reporter from the *Universe*, seeing his chance for a world scoop, took a photograph. His flash gun frightened the Donkey so much that this time the Donkey peed on stage and St Joseph, standing to make his exit, slipped in it. As St Joseph slipped, his foot came out of his costume, the crêpe-paper beard fell off and he stood up six foot tall, clean-featured and handsome,

looking for all the world as though he had been reborn.

'A miracle!' screamed my Grandmother. 'Be de powers of de Lord God,'tis a blessed miracle! De humpty-back choild's been cured!'

At this point the headmaster woke up. 'Down periscope,' he screamed, 'take her down to fifty fathoms and stop all engines.'

4

We Are The Mystery Riders

We are the mystery riders,
We fight the spiders from off the wall.

I believed so much in the things that I saw at the cinema when I was eight years old or so that I became to all intents and purposes a miniature Catholic cowboy, somewhere between Hopalong Cassidy and the Holy Ghost. My Grandmother was the sheriff, a role she didn't mind playing as it left her firmly in command. Because I, as Holy Hopalong Cassidy, did most of the work she spent all her time – like most good sheriffs do – in the rocking chair on the porch of the peg rug that was her jailhouse, saying her rosary. My enemies were 'the Devil and all his works', according to my Gran, but since the only works I knew were the dye-works at the bottom of the hill I assumed that hell was a gigantic sort of factory where the Devil kept sinners at work. When I left school and got my first job in a factory I was to discover that I wasn't far wrong.

My weapons against the Devil were two cap pistols from Woolworth's, total price (including belt, holster, felt cowboy hat, waistcoat and leggings) three shillings and sixpence, a king's ransom in those days when you could get a woman and a hot pie for two shillings. Mind you, the pies – as the poet once said – weren't up to much.

'What does the Devil look like?' I asked my Grandmother one day.

'Auld Nick, choild? Begod and bless us and save us, but he's de wickedest ting you could ever see. Sure and he's got de two horns on his head, a long tail and de cloven hoofs on his feet like an auld billy goat. His eyes are just slits in his head and he can see right trew you and tell every mortal ting ye'd be thinkin'. And he's so clever, begod! He'd blaggard you out of yer immortal soul in five minutes.'

One night, coming home from the 'fil-ums', as my Grandmother used to call them, with my friend Wharfie I saw the Devil under the gaslamp at the corner of our street. In reality, the Devil was no one more diabolical than Old Man

Dwyer, a local drunk who was coming home steaming from the Buffaloes – the working-class equivalent of the Masons. He was carrying the buffalo horns on his head, and doing the okey cokey on his own at the bus stop, when Wharfie and I ran out at him with cap guns blazing away, giving Red Indian yells. He threw the horns over the chip shop wall and ran screaming into church shouting for Monsignor McGuinness to hear his confession. Ever after that Old Man Dwyer never touched a drop of drink, swearing that Chester's bitter, known locally as 'lunatic soup', had given him the DTs. Wharfie and I, in the mean time, were convinced we'd vanquished the Devil if not for ever then at least for a time and went back to more temporal enemies.

'The Johnson Boys have hit town', I muttered, riding round the table on an imaginary white steed one day.

'Begob! Dem blaggards. I thought yez had dem all killed yesterday.'

'These are their brothers!'

'Begob, dey must be Catlicks den. It's a hell of a size of a family dey have.'

I took my Grandmother with me to the pictures once and vowed that never again would I go with her. During the B-movie, a cowboy film, she cheered the baddies and booed the goodies and when the lady came round with the ice-cream tray she got into a row with her about the cost of the ice cream.

'Begob, is it chargin' that much ye are? Come on out o'dat would yez! Ye'd steal the eye from my head and come back for the socket!'

When the feature film, *Flash Gordon on the Planet of Loose Women,* came on, all was well until three of Emperor Ming's lady captives appeared on the screen wearing tunics and tights, and showing a lot of leg.

'Love of God!' screamed my Grandmother, slamming her seat back and hitting four rows above and below with her whirling rosary beads. 'Is dis de kind of ting yez'd be showin' to a Catlick grandmother and her grandchoild?'

When an ice-cream lady waved her torch at her and told her to shut up, my Grandmother knocked her over – showering the people in the ninepennies with choc ice and Orange Maids and the manager (who knew what was good for him) ran up the aisle and locked himself in his office.

All the way home on the bus my Grandmother muttered and grumbled about what she had seen. 'Begob, dem hussies,' she told the bus aloud in a voice that would have been at home sounding through the fog across the Mersey bar. 'It's no wonder dis country lost India! What wid de *News of de World* – dat whoor's gazette! And den dem women on de fil-ums showin' all dere timbers! Begob, it's toime Oirland stopped sendin' nurses and butter to dis unholy place!' I suffered the journey in silence while people all around me tapped the sides of their heads and made knowing winks.

It was not long after that, that the great Irk flood took place and my Grandmother was able to use her canoe for the first and only time. Freed of having to provide fish for the dugong, my Grandfather had got a job as a night watchman in a factory that made parkin and tripe-flavoured crisps, a great favourite in the northern pubs at that time. One morning he came home from work rather late. My Gran had had his favourite dish of cockroach soup and rat *au poivre* warming in a bucket on the stove for some time when he burst through the door, his face the colour of old cod.

'Begob! De river's up and risin'!' he cried. 'It's been risin' all night since dem heavy rains we've had, and dere's a blockage in de Ship Canal. One of de day shift men said de floods've already washed away de hot pie stall down be de bus station.'

'Dat's it!' cried my Grandmother, throwing down the copy

of *Lives of the Saints* that she was knitting. 'Grandmothers and children first!'

We commandeered a passing ragman's cart and together wheeled the canoe down to the river. It was indeed rising. The once-sluggish stream barely twelve feet wide, and usually all the colours of the rainbow from the dye factory up the road, was now a fast-flowing torrent at least three feet deep, with real swirls and eddies. I had recently been reading *Huckleberry Finn* and now here I was, setting out on my own Mississippi with my very own Tom Sawyer sitting in the prow of the canoe, her St Christopher medal pinned to the eagle's nose, her paddle flashing in the evening sunlight.

After four hundred yards we ran aground on a shoal of milk crates, old prams and half-sunken pianos that weren't marked on the chart.

'We'll hang on here till de water rises enough to float us off,' she said as the first stars of night began to smoulder above the

coke works. 'Dis puts me in mind', she said, 'of an auld song written be Willie Clancey, de fella who used to come round and light de gas lamps in our street,' and she burst into song before I could stop her.

> Twas a wild and windy blustery night,
>   When we set sail all three,
>   Me and Paddy and Mick MacPhew,
>   All bound for Timbucthree.

>   Riddley, iddley, diddley dee.

>   A blustery wind blew wild that night,
>   And filled the toilet paper sails,
>   And Mad Mick sat atop the mast,
>   A-chewin' on his nails.

>   Riddley, iddley, diddley dee.

>   'All hands on deck' the captain cried,
>   His breath was comin' in lumps,
>   'All hands on deck and dem with no hands,
>   Yez can all throw up yer stumps.'

>   Riddley, iddley, diddley dee.

She sang on in this fashion till morning when the sunlight rising over the glue factory found us stranded on an island of junk in the middle of what was once again a muddy creek. The rats came out to laugh at us, rolling on their backs in the mud with their paws in the air. We suffered this indignity until the fire brigade came, and two of the strongest firemen waded through the ooze to carry us and the canoe back to shore.

'Watch where you're putting yer hands, young man! Dis is a Catlick woman you've got hold of here! Not some auld biddy dat doesn't know de difference between bein' rescued and bein' ravished.'

'Leave it out, Ma,' said the fireman. 'I'm young enough to be your son.'

'Me son, is it? If you was me son den I'd have yez stop drinkin' and cut yer fingernails. Yer breath smells like Boddingtons' brewery and ye've torn holes in me liberty bodice wid yer claws.'

When we got home my Grandfather was sitting by the fire, with a toasting fork and some crumpets. 'How was de floods?' he asked, winking at me with one eye.

'Ye'll be laughin' on de other side of yer face when de flood does come again and dere's nobody saved but me and de choild.'

We sat by the fire and ate our crumpets. The dog lay on the hearthrug in the firelight, eyes closed, his legs going round like those of a trick cyclist.

'What in God's name is he doin'?' asked my Grandad.

'He's chasin' rabbits in his sleep,' said my Gran.

'Well, I wish to God he'd catch de buggers in his sleep, he's gettin' on me bloody nerves.'

There was a knock at the door. My Grandad got up and let McClusky in. McClusky the one-armed window cleaner and uncle of Bernadette, the jelly baby queen, was a regular visitor at our house. Every Wednesday evening he would come round for a game of whist and a bottle of Guinness with my Grandfather and Grandmother. He came through the door with his flat hat perched rakishly over one ear and a toffee cigarette in his mouth.

My Uncle Bernard looked up from the tablecloth he was reading. 'It says here that a man called Hilary has just climbed Everest with a sherpa called Tensing.'

'Begob. You wouldn't get me up a mountain wid a man called Hilary,' snorted my Grandad. 'I wouldn't trust any man wid de name of Hilary. I bet dat little sherpa climbed de hill backwards.'

'You've got a bad mind,' said my Grandmother, 'and in front of de choild too!'

'Begob and you wouldn't say dat if you saw some of dem British army officers dancing wid each other after lights out, shouting "Huzzah, boys, huzzah!" and doin' de lancers to a wind-up gramophone or forcing some poor Oirish swaddy to accompany dem on de mouth organ or de jew's harp. I used to pray dat Jerry would send a whizz-bang on top of de lot of dem. I was hopin' to see de headlines in de newspapers: "Whizz-Bang Bangs Puffs".'

'If you'd been brought up at one of dem public schools yez might have ended up like that,' said my Grandmother.

'Dat's a load of hokum,' said my Grandad, and he snorted. 'If – huh! If me aunt had balls she'd be me uncle.'

My Grandfather was full of sayings like this, such as 'a wet shilling is better than a dry halfpenny.' 'Don't kick the dog up the bum when you've got your fingers in his mouth.' And his favourite, one that he used over and over again, 'De Oirish are de white blacks of Europe.' He said it again on this particular evening and McClusky, looking up from his hand full of aces said, 'Talkin' about blacks, I hear dat some of dem darkies are said to be very well provided when it comes to de wedding tackle. I hear de generative organs are of a considerable size.'

'Well, I knew de wan dat had wan dat took two men to carry,' hinted my Grandad, obtusely.

'D'you tell me dat now?'

'I do surely. It had de handles specially fixed to it and a mirror to look behind you.'

'Love of God! Dat must have been a tremenjuice organ altogether!'

'It was more of a harmonium type of class of yoke. Wan of dem tings wid de bellas dat yez work wid yer feet.'

'Begob, I thought you was talking about another class of organ altogether.'

'Not at all! What do I know about darkies' mickeys? D'yez tink I'd go round askin' a man for a look at his mickey and him a stranger? I can see meself doin' it, I don't tink! "Good evenin' dere, sir. A fine night it's turned out in de end. Would yez ever give us a look at yer auld mickey now?" Begob, not even doctors look at yer mickey.'

'D'ye tell me dat now?'

'I do surely. When a doctor looks at you all he sees is plumbing. As far as he's concerned it's not a mickey, it's an overflow wid a stop cock.'

'But how about de other function of de mickey?' asked McClusky, puzzled.

'Begob man, dat's nutten to do wid yer doctor! Dat's between you, yer creator and yer parish priest and I don't intend to discuss de secrets of de confessional wid a man who's stupid enough to tink dat all darkies have big mickies. That's like sayin' dat all Protestants have tails.'

'And so dey do,' shouted McClusky.

'Well, I only ever saw de one Protestant wid no clothes on and she was on a rug at de time so it could have been de fringe of de rug and not a tail at all.'

'What were you doin' wid a Protestant woman on a rug?'

'I was tryin' to convert her to de one true faith.'

'Did you confess it afterwards at all?'

'Sure and wasn't I doing de church's work, and besides if it's not a Catlick girl it's only a venial sin.'

'And did it work?'

'It did but only for a while till a Buddhist fella wid a better class of converter had her burnin' incense, bangin' gongs and wearin' a yellow nightie widdin two weeks.'

It was in this year, Coronation year, that I began to dream of meeting the Queen and joined the Mystery Riders. The two things are totally disconnected but are probably worth recording – even if only that at some later date they may be called up in evidence in a court of law. Our neighbourhood was bristling with gangs at that time. There was the Green Hand Gang who lived on Factory Brew. They were dedicated to mayhem, riot and stealing milk bottles off doorsteps. They also bashed up kids from other gangs, and painted a green hand on the kids they'd bashed up as a sign that they had been so dealt with. The Red Devils were from further into town, in amongst the murky streets of close-packed houses by the river and the rubber stick-on sole factory, where even the police dogs went round in pairs. The Red Devils were experts at safe-breaking, forgery and hijacking grocery delivery bikes. They were a force much to be feared. The Silver Eagle Gang from the posher end of our little world was largely composed of softies. Their forte was chasing pigeons, flicking up girls' skirts so they could see their knickers, and shouting after men on bicycles such witticisms as 'Ey, Mistor! Your wheels are gowin' rownd!'

The Mystery Riders, however, were like none of these. We were in a class of our own. In our gang there was Bunny, myself, Wharfie, Woodie and Tomo. We met in a patch of wasteland behind the garage on the main road, and in an old Lion brand exercise book we signed our names in blood and vowed to be true even unto death.

No band of Freemasons ever went through a more gruelling initiation ceremony than that devised by the Mystery Riders. Firstly you had to sign your name in blood. Getting a little spot out of your thumb was not enough for us – we wanted an inkwell full. Bunny, who had been drummed out of the Silver Eagle Gang for being seen holding hands with a girl coming home from the pictures, fainted when Woodie drew the cheese

grater across his thumb.

Once you'd signed your name you had to perform three tasks, beside which the tasks of Hercules looked like a day off. You had to:

1 Kick an Alsatian (and it had to have a full set of teeth and be totally mobile).

2 Stay in the haunted house on your own while the rest of the gang counted up to a thousand.

3 Blindfolded, steal an apple from the tree in the school caretaker's garden.

The Alsatian-kicking wasn't too difficult, at least for the first one or two of the gang. It was a big Alsatian belonging to a local policeman but after Wharfie and I had kicked it, it merely looked puzzled and faintly annoyed. Then when Tomo kicked it, it tore the backside out of his trousers. By the time Woodie kicked it, it knew the score and pretended not to notice until he turned away – when it sank its teeth into his bum. If Woodie hadn't had his catapult in his back pocket the dog would have had bum *au naturelle* for lunch.

Bunny kicked it and spent the night on the coal shed roof.

The haunted house was an empty house on the other side of the park where all the houses had gardens, cellars and attics and were very, very old and creepy. This one stood alone and crumbling in its own grounds, the roof and windows still intact – but only just. It had been empty for years and was said to be haunted by a headless cavalier, a mad woman who drank children's blood and a phantom rag and bone man who clip-clopped round the garden with his horse and cart shining white on moonlit nights shouting 'Rag bone! Any old iron! Balloons for rags!' in a tremulous ghostly voice.

On the night of the full moon, the Mystery Riders made their way to the haunted house and one after the other we climbed in through the cellar and counted each other out. I said forty Our Fathers, forty Hail Marys, a perfect Act of Contrition and vowed never to sin ever again if only God would let me out of this alive. Bunny came off worst. We were just getting to 991 on the count when some members of the Green Hand Gang came round the corner. Knowing what was good for us, we scarpered in the general direction of off. The Green Hand Gang, drunk on sarsaparilla from the Temperance Bar, climbed into the haunted house. Bunny, thinking that they were ghosts after him, screamed like a banshee and ran off upstairs in the darkened house – dashing into a cupboard in mistake for a door. The cupboard had a big bag of white distemper powder in it. Its rotten sides caved in as Bunny kicked it, covering himself from head to foot in white powder. Turning blindly out of the cupboard, he ran back down through the house. Running through the Green Hand Gang came a wailing snivelling ghost, and jumping out of the windows, crying for their mothers, came the Green Hand Gang.

The school caretaker had one crabby apple tree growing in the middle of a sooty garden where broken window frames leaned drunkenly over miserable damp-looking lettuce. The plague of his very existence were the gangs of lads who climbed his wall, day in and day out, to steal sooty sour apples that gave them belly-ache and the runs before they'd even finished eating them. The school caretaker was one of the old school who believed in giving you a good clout if he caught you, rather than telling your parents. All of us wandered blindfold into the biggest hidings of our lives.

The aims of the Mystery Riders gang were to avenge wrongs, to fight evil and injustice wherever we found it, and to pick up any washing we'd found that had fallen down off the clothes lines stretched across the back streets of our town. The last idea was Tomo's, because he had once done just this and been given sixpence by an old lady for picking her washing up from the puddles into which it had fallen. For a week we scoured the streets looking for evil-doers, injustice and fallen washing. The only evil we saw was a man hitting a dog and when we went to rescue the dog it tried to bite us. The lack of fallen washing was a bit of a disappointment. Finally Tomo and Wharfie went ahead of the gang knocking it down, and the rest of us followed on picking it up. Before we were rumbled we made thirty shillings and spent all the money on sweets and the rowing boats on the park lake. In the middle of the lake, Bunny got drunk on wine gums and declared that he could walk on water. We found out not only that he couldn't walk on water but that he couldn't even swim. Luckily the lake was only three feet deep where he fell in – so after screaming and splashing and swallowing gallons of muddy weedy evil-smelling water he staggered on to the banks and squelched home crying, as we lay helpless with laughter in the bottom of the boat.

I was at this time deeply puzzled by all things religious. If God was everywhere, as I had been told, then why didn't people trip over him? I asked Monsignor McGuinness this once when he came round to give us a catechism test. This happened once a year, and made the Spanish inquisition look like the Stork and butter test. If we all knew our catechism answers then the Monsignor told Mr Parker, the headmaster, to give us a half-day holiday and we all shouted 'three cheers for Monsignor McGuinness'. It was about as spontaneous as the Nuremburg rally, the only difference being that we didn't run out and invade Poland afterwards.

When Monsignor McGuinness came round in the year of the Mystery Riders, we almost lost the half-day holiday because John Yates had failed miserably the question on the Ten Commandments, falling down on the Fourth Commandment which he said was 'Thou shalt not piddle in the bath'. I'd put my hand up and answered them all correctly and seemingly reprieved the half-day. I put my hand up again as the sigh of relief died down around the classroom and asked, 'Please, Monsignor, if God is everywhere why don't we trip over him?'

'Ah,' he said quick as a flash, his eleven chins wobbling like a blancmange staircase, 'God is everywhere in a spiritual – not a temporal – sense, if you have my meaning. According to St Augustine, he's there but not there.'

Somebody behind me whispered, 'Just like Batman and Robin.' But I ignored it.

That afternoon, still puzzled by the answer, I wound up the hearing aid and asked my Grandmother why, if God was everywhere, we didn't keep tripping up over him. 'Monsignor McGuinness says it's because he's with us in a spiritual, not a temporal, sense.'

'Dat's a load of old mullarky, if you'll pardon me French. De reason we don't trip up over God is dat as well as bein' everywhere he's also omniscient, dat is yer man God sees everyting and gets out of de way before yez can trip over him.'

Another question had puzzled me for some time and, seeing that my Grandmother seemed to be something of a pundit when it came to matters almighty, I asked her, 'If God can do anything he wants, why doesn't he stop all the wrong and wicked things in the world?'

She thought for a moment and then said, 'Because, son – God is a heavy drinker.'

The thing that got me into most trouble was my guardian angel, a misunderstanding that started one night in the kitchen: I had my cowboy suit on, having been galloping round the streets all day looking for evil to fight and finding none, my Uncle Bernard was reading the tablecloth while Uncle Harry was working on a machine that would turn him into a millionaire overnight. My Grandfather was sitting by the fire, smoking his pipe and nodding before the flames. He looked up and rubbed the side of his nose with one finger, croaking, 'Could yez knit me a book at all? I've nearly finished dis wan.'

'What sort of a book would you be wantin'?' asked my Grandmother.

'A cowboy book would be nice to have now for de readin'.'

'Tanks be to Jaysus yez don't want another detective book. Some of dem Agatha Christies is terrible hard to knit.'

I was on my way upstairs to bed when my Grandmother looked sideways at me and shouted, 'Don't forget to say a special prayer to your guardian angel.' I misheard her totally and knelt down that night by the side of my bed, hands together, eyes closed, and prayed for ten minutes to my gardening angel. The next morning after assembly Miss Worswick asked us all if we'd said our prayers the night before. I put my hand up, and with the kind of stupidity bred only from innocence and optimism told Miss Worswick that I'd said a special prayer the night before for my gardening angel. A board duster backed with mahogany sped across the room at the speed of light.

'You fool,' she screeched, 'guardian angel not gardening angel.'

At that moment, the vision of legions of angels with hoes and rakes wandering around paradise settling the clouds into neat piles and ridges vanished from my mind completely.

'What is a guardian angel, please Miss Worswick?' I asked.

'Your guardian angel,' she said, 'goes everywhere with you. He loves you and looks after you. He's sent especially from God to help you when temptation comes and when the Devil comes to tempt you to sin.'

'I've never seen my guardian angel, Miss Worswick,' I said, 'where is he?'

'Your guardian angel,' said Miss Worswick, 'is everywhere with you. Wherever you go your guardian angel will be there at your side.'

Michael Coffee put his hand up. 'Please, Miss Worswick, what does our guardian angel look like?'

'Well,' said Miss Worswick, 'your guardian angel is tall with long golden hair and wears a beautiful silver gown. He has great white feathery wings on his back, so that he can fly through the air, and he's very tall and very handsome and he's invisible.'

Again, with an ignorance bred only from optimism and stupidity, my hand shot up from amongst a forest of bewildered and uncomprehending faces. 'Please, Miss Worswick,' I asked, digging my grave with my mouth, 'how do you know what the guardian angels look like if they're invisible?' Again the board rubber shot across the room, catching me this time on the side of my ear and ricocheting off

to hit Bernadette McClusky on the back of the head.

From then on, convinced that the guardian angel went everywhere with me, I paid for him on the bus, refused to let anyone sit next to me in case they sat on him and would only go to the toilet with the light out. One day we were playing football on one of the bomb sites that still littered Manchester and I was in goal between two piles of coats, when Wharfie came behind the goal to have a pee. He hitched up the leg of his shorts and began making patterns in the dust with his widdle when all of a sudden he burst into tears.

'What's up, Wharfie?' I asked, puzzled at seeing one of the hard men of the gang crying so dementedly.

He turned to me with red-rimmed eyes and in a sob cried out, 'I think I've just piddled on my guardian angel.'

The Mystery Riders were eventually disbanded on the orders of the police after the events at the Conservative garden party and, though we carried on for a number of months as an underground organisation modelled on the French maquis, we never really functioned properly as a unit after that. The case of the Conservative garden party never made the headlines, although it should have done. It's my belief that the story was suppressed by the powers that be to protect some of those in very high places. There has sprung up over the years a conspiracy theory, and a second donkey theory, but perhaps the truth may never be known.

The Mystery Riders had been infiltrated by a boy called Simon Lensky whose father ran an army surplus store that stood on the corner of our street where it met the main road. Lensky, or 'Brains' as he was known, was a highly intelligent nine-year-old anarcho-syndicalist who believed that all government is bad government – and as the years have gone by I've come to realise the truth of that simplistic statement only too well.

He converted us all to the cause of anarchy one night as we sat smoking tea-leaves in Lensky's back kitchen. His mother and father were out at a whist drive in the local church hall and Lensky and the Mystery Riders were experimenting with drugs. We found that smoking tea-leaves wrapped in newspaper gave us about two seconds of bright-coloured lights and voices in our ears before we threw up. We were persevering and trying for the three-second buzz. Some of the harder cases in the mob had 'gotten into' sniffing custard powder. The results were extreme giddiness, the ability to talk to stones and the formation of the brightest and yellowest boogies known to medical science. It was later that evening, as we lay sprawled round the carpet looking at his collection of *Radio Fun* comics, that Lensky dropped an intellectual bombshell into our midst.

'The role of the worker has always been that of pawn in wartime, a pool of brute physical force and labour in peacetime, but above all as a consumer not so much for capitalist society as for whatever government is in power at the time.'

Tomo, who was a pure Marxist-Leninist with faintly revisionist tendencies when it came to the redistribution of Walls' ice cream, grew red in the face and blurted out, 'When the workers gain complete control of the means of production, and when society is based upon the abilities and needs of all within it, and when the conspiracy of international capitalism has finally brought about its own downfall, then there will be no talk of pawns or pools of labour, all men will be free!'

'And who,' asked Lensky sagely, sucking a gobstopper and flicking over a page of Abbott and Costello cartoons, 'will empty the dustbins and repair the sewers – the politicians?'

Tomo was silent.

'The Stalinist purges are less the result of pressure from the

81

capitalist world outside the USSR than the need of all
governments, communist or otherwise, to destroy liberty
within the nation. A government will only allow its people
that liberty that it sees fit. So long as there are governors and
governed, there will never be freedom – never, *never*,
NEVER.' And Lensky banged the table so hard his cup of
Camp coffee fell over.

The rest of us jumped to our feet and gave him a standing
ovation. Even Tomo grudgingly pulled himself up off the
carpet and put his hands together.

That night we plotted the overthrow of the three main
political parties in Britain.

'We need bombs,' said Tomo.

'And tanks and aeroplanes,' said Wharfie.

'Can't we just begin by shouting dirty words through their
letter-boxes?' said Bunny, who was already beginning to get
cold feet.

'We have to start with a policy of disruption,' said Lensky. 'This is the classic anarchist strategy. You pursue a policy of disruption until the populace has become discontented and more of the proletariat flock to the anarchist cause. We'll begin our campaign by disrupting the Conservative garden party that is due to take place this Saturday,' and he rose to his feet, brandishing a spearmint chew, crying, 'Long live the anarcho-syndicalists of Crumpsall and the Mystery Riders Gang.' And to a man we echoed his words.

Within the next few days we managed to get hold of a programme for the forthcoming junket. There were to be hoop-la stalls, a bran tub, a brass band, a Miss Britannia competition, fancy dress, a coconut shy, donkey rides and a speech by some lady called Smithers-Green-Brown-Green who was married to some low-ranking Tory Minister, a sort of second reserve in the Ministry of Foods.

As the day approached, our plans crystallised. We were going to put crabs in the bran tub, glue on the coconuts, let loose rats in the tent where the Miss Britannia competitors would be changing, and we were going to suck lemons in front of the brass band and doctor the donkey's feed-bag. In the event our plans worked out better than any of us could have prayed for had we spent several months of Sundays on our knees.

The garden party was taking place in the grounds at the rear of the local Conservative club. As we arrived that sunny Saturday morning the brass band were unpacking their instruments and the first guests were arriving, the women all twin sets and pearls, bosoms stiffly-brassiered and buttocks tightly-corseted, teeth like tiled walls and eyes like gimlets; the men stiff-legged, besuited and razor-mouthed, exchanging masonic handshakes like naughty boys swapping sweets under the eyes of a watchful teacher.

The plan was simple. Over a loudspeaker system a record player was playing Colonel Bogey. Bunny was to capture the microphone tent and cause a diversion with an announcement. In the mêlée that followed we would place all our props and booby traps. Behind the stalls, permed and rinsed, the necks of their blouses held firmly in place by giant brooches, stood a regiment of Tory ladies trying to ape the antics of fairground barkers and failing miserably because of their accents. Where a barker would have shouted, 'Come on, now, let's 'ave yer! Tanner for three throws! Everyone a prize! A goldfish for yer Gran now – that's a fair swap int it?', the ladies like school ma'ams jollying along slow readers were calling in horsey tones, 'Only sixpence for three throws at the coconuts – good afternoon, vicar, how nice to see you. Lovely day! Come along now, it's all in a good cause – little boy' (to me) 'wouldn't you like a chance of winning a coconut?'

Brains gave Bunny the nod, and he slipped into the microphone tent. The record, 'Riding Along on the Crest of a Wave', ended with a sudden scratching tearing noise and Bunny's voice, deliberately gruffened and deepened to sound like a man's but sounding more like Micky Mouse with laryngitis, said, 'Ladies and gentlemen, can I have your attention please. Somebody has dropped a £50 note on the lawn. Will you please look around you and if you find it bring it over to the judges' tent.'

In the confusion that followed all the wicked deeds were done. The glue was set on the base of the coconuts, the crabs dropped in the bran tub, the rats let loose in the changing tent and the donkey's feed-bag dosed with a bottle of liquid paraffin and some mushy peas we'd bought from the chip shop the night before. At a signal from Brains, Tomo started off a rumour that the money had been found and, with a groan, five hundred brothers and sisters of monetarism got up off their knees and the bacchanalia continued.

Wharfie, Tomo and I wandered over to where the brass band was beginning to play. Halfway through a Sousa march Tomo, a giant lemon covering his face, stood in front of the band sucking loudly and sounding like a sink plunger on overtime. It is a well-known fact that it is impossible for a brass player to blow his instrument while somebody is sucking a lemon in front of him. The first player to notice Tomo was the lead cornet player who, in the middle of a spirited solo passage, produced a strangled squeal, then nothing else as his lips acting with a will of their own puckered and winced at the sight of Tomo slurping at the lemon. The trombone player played a glissando fart, while the E flat bass player hit a note that sounded like a flatulent water buffalo mating in a pond.

The conductor turned around and, seeing Tomo, chased him off the brass band playing area with his stick. He came back to the bandstand grim-faced, sweating and breathless, just as a shriek tore the air and a woman with a crab on her finger did a back flip on to a table loaded with cakes and pastries. She landed heavily on one end, catapulting a hail of custard creams, cups of tea and flakey pastries all over the field. At the coconut stall a policeman stood red-faced and embarrassed as a crying boy and his mother demonstrated a blatant act of fraud perpetrated by the ladies of the local Conservative Party.

The fancy dress procession was simultaneously making its way round the field toward the judges' table. A variety of Micky Mice, Plutos, devils, gorillas, Shirley Temples, Marilyn Monroes, Charlie Chaplins, Winston Churchills and tramps picked their way through a morass of cakes and churned-up lawn, their members swelled by several real tramps brought in from the street by Wharfie who'd told them about the first prize of £5 and a bottle of tonic wine. Under the influence of methylated spirits they meandered towards the judges, moving as though in a dream. At the judges' table the procession stopped.

A cough travelled round the field from the tannoys fixed on to the poles and trees, and a half-demented voice asked no one in particular, 'Is it on? Can they hear me? Is it working? I've never used one of these bally things before. Testing, hello, testing. Ladies and gentlemen, can you hear me at the back? Thank you? Yes, thank you. Ahem – ladies and gentlemen, I would like on behalf of Crumpsall Conservative Party to welcome you all to our annual summer fair. We do so hope you will enjoy yourselves.'

The words were coming from the slit in the face that passed for the mouth of a large lady who bred bulldogs, and had come over the years to so resemble her charges that while tying her laces one day she had been patted on the head and given a biscuit by a passerby. She droned on in a voice that made dogs for miles around slink under tables, tails drooping.

'I would now like to cordially invite to officially open our gala the Right Honourable Mrs Smithers-Green-Brown-Green, the wife of our Under-Minister for Potatoes.'

There was a small spatter of applause, and a very large lady built like a hippopotamus got to her feet. At her side was her husband, a bald lean man with a thin moustache on his lip that made him look as though he had been drinking soot. His good lady held a sheaf of papers in her hand.

'Ladies and gentlemen,' she began, in a voice that rose and fell in shrill intensity like somebody sawing tin on a swing. 'It is so nice to see that today when the Socialists have done so much to destroy things that we hold dear in our country that at least they haven't managed to destroy the weather.'

There was a muffled titter, somebody at the back of the crowd booed, and was hit by a man with spats and a shooting stick. As she burbled on, the poor patient donkey – he of the

86

tribe that had carried the mother of God on his back to Bethlehem and later carried her son himself over palm leaves through the city of Jerusalem – was passing behind the judges' table with a little girl on its back. The mushy peas and liquid paraffin were beginning to work for, as the Right Honourable Mrs Smithers-Green-Brown-Green turned over her pages, the ass rent the air with a crescendo of amazingly loud farts. 'Hear, hear,' shouted one of the tramps. The Mystery Riders on the edge of the crowd were on their knees in painful silent mirth. A single solitary fart ricocheted from the rear of the Conservative club and echoed round the field.

'Thunder,' said one deaf old lady, looking aloft into a cloudless summer sky.

'That woman's got a very bad cough,' said another.

'Begob,' said Molly, who was a staunch Tory and had turned up for the day, 'the smell of that woman's breath would make a badger bald.'

On the judges' table things were not going well. The lady with a face like a bulldog, her nose wrinkled in disgust, was glaring at the Honourable Mr Smithers-Green-Brown-Green as though he had done something unspeakable. His wife, red-faced and unsure of herself, was about to carry on with her speech when a fart to end all farts blew her notes out of her hand and across the field in a shower of foolscap. Totally lost now, she looked at the sea of uncomprehending faces before her, most of whom couldn't understand how this lady – though large – was producing such enormous explosions, nor could they understand why she had suddenly thrown a pile of papers into the air. She looked at the fancy dress parade before her and in panic shouted, 'The decision of the judges is that the third prize of five shillings goes to Noddy and Big Ears, the second prize of ten shillings jointly to Winston Churchill and Marilyn Monroe and the first prize of £5 and a bottle of tonic wine goes to the tramp.'

There were twenty-seven tramps on the lawn, and when the first prize was awarded to the only tramp that wasn't real the inevitable happened. A large gentleman of the road with wild ginger hair, mad eyes and clothes so ragged he looked as though he had been struck by lightning, grabbed the pretend tramp, a costing accountant in the local Town Hall parks and cemeteries department and, lifting him up by the throat, snarled in a broad Glaswegian accent, 'Seeyouse Jemmey! Yer deed soyare! Yarra fuin' bassa ahm gonakillyez!' And he swung a punch that missed completely and broke the nose of a tramp behind who'd fallen asleep standing up, and who now woke to find the view from one of his eyes blocked by his nostrils.

Tramps everywhere began hitting each other all over the field, people not wishing to be left out or appear spoilsports joined in. Several screams crossed the field from the Miss Britannia changing tent, unnoticed in the general maelstrom of curses, wails and the sounds of people falling down. From the tent streamed a gaggle of semi-hysterical Britannias in various states of unreadiness. One plump one tripped over her shield and goosed Winston Churchill with her trident, while a well-endowed Britannia wearing little but her underwear and her helmet stood in a pile of cream cakes and tea screaming – and when Noddy tried to console her hit him so hard he knocked the Hunchback of Notre Dame into Donald Duck.

'Begob,' said Molly, ''tis better than the fil-ums.'

The Honourable Mrs Smithers-Green-Brown-Green, now totally hysterical, tried to step down from the dais aided by her husband. The donkey had become so disturbed by the noise that it had kicked itself free from its owners and was braying loudly and indignantly, with its dangerous end pointed towards the approaching judges. Unheeding the early warnings the donkey had been recently giving, the judges trudged tearfully towards it. It is universally acknowledged that those muscles which a donkey uses to bray are linked very closely with those muscles which a donkey uses to defecate. This donkey had been dosed with a mixture which rendered its internal workings as volatile and as dangerous as a New Zealand mud geyser, and as the party of six high-ranking officials approached there was a bray, a bang and a swarm of what looked like brown bees in a dun-coloured fog enveloped the judges. Six blind gingerbread men and women staggered out of the other side of the fog, some crying, some coughing, but all of them very unhappy.

It was at that point that the Mystery Riders, about to make their escape, were grabbed by the policeman who had previously been seen at the coconut shy.

'How did you know it was us?' asked Brains, suspended two foot off the air by his shirt collar.

'Nobody else round here,' said the policeman, 'has ever bought ten shillings worth of mushy peas at a time.'

5

Dib, Dib, Dib, Dub, Dub, Dub, Our Akela's Up The Tub

When I was nine or so I joined the Cubs. I wasn't too sure about joining because I knew it to be a paramilitary organisation – but one of my mates told me that if you joined the Cubs you did exciting things like abseiling down cliffs and parachuting out of aeroplanes. He'd actually got mixed up with an advert he'd seen for the Royal Marine Commandos, but we'd already signed up with the Cubs for the duration by the time we'd found out that we'd let ourselves in for nothing more exciting than tree identification, camp-fire songs and growing hyacinths for our gardener's badge.

When my Grandmother found out, she was furious, equating the Cubs with some junior branch of the British Army.

'It's only for fun!' I told her.

'Would yous come on out of dat. D'yous tink I was borned

yesterday? Before yer know it ye'll be across de water shootin' poor Oirishmen!'

'I won't, Gran,' I cried, 'it's only for us to go camping and hiking and that.'

But she was unswerving. 'Not at all,' she muttered. 'What koind of an organisation is it at all dat takes children and teaches dem to shoot der cousins and uncles? Michael' (and she pulled me towards her) 'if you hear dat de British are about to re-invade Oireland den don't forget to tell me, would yez? I'll write to yer Uncle Barney and tell him to hide de pigs. De buggers requisitioned dem durin' de Troubles and gave him an IOU and when he tried to get it paid de man laughed him out of court cos de fly divils had signed it "Charlie Chaplin".'

When I came home wearing my green uniform she was puzzled. 'Is it St Patrick's Day already?' she muttered, squinting at the calendar.

'No, it's my uniform,' I shouted, cranking the hearing aid.

'Begob, it must be some branch of the Oirish army you've joined! Dere's hope for yez yet.'

Not long afterwards my Grandmother stopped knitting books. 'Sacred heart of Jaysus!' she cried one day, 'de filthy language I'm having to knit dese days! Ye wouldn't believe it! All dis kitchen sink stuff! Begob, we know what de kitchen sink looks like without having our noses rubbed in it!'

'It's literature,' said my Uncle Bernard, who was something of an artist. 'It's great art you're talking about there.'

'Literature, is it? Dat D.H. Lawrence wid all his talk of mickeys and I don't know what! Art is it? I'd rather have a paintin' of a bowl of flowers dan a paintin' of a mickey any day. I seen pictures of some of dem statues be dat Michael Angelo fella and as far as I'm concerned dey'd be better off wid deir trousers on.'

'What's all dis talk of mickeys?' asked my Grandfather, coming in from the kitchen where he'd been ironing the Dover sole flat for tea. 'D'yez not know dere's a choild in de house and it's soon enough he'll be findin' out about de ways of de world without yous putting ideas into his head.'

'I can't hear a word yer sayin',' muttered my Grandmother who used this as a ploy every time she didn't want to be involved in an argument.

'Can't hear, is it?' shouted my Grandad, cranking up the generator. 'Well I'll bloody soon make you hear.' And he began to wind the handle so fast that his arm became a blur and the resulting electrical storm blew the speakers out of every radio for streets around, cutting Ronnie Renald off in the middle of whistling 'If I Was a Blackbird' on the Billy Cotton Band Show.

The end result of it all was that my Grandmother stopped knitting books, and instead developed an interest in music. She had for a long time owned a xylophone which she kept in one corner of the room, but although she tuned it carefully each day she'd never learnt to play it, using it instead as a filing system for her collection of great toasted bread slices of the world.

It's always difficult living in a small house with somebody who's trying to learn a musical instrument and my Grandmother's attempts to become a jazz drummer were particularly trying. The drum kit she was practising on was a mongrel affair, a hotch-potch of garnered percussive items that, when collected together, looked like an accident in a plumber's shop. The bass drum had come via an old Salvation Army band and had 'Jesus Saves' painted on it. The snare drum was a Boys' Brigade marching drum and the tom toms were two African talking drums made from clay, raffia and water buffalo hide, and the first time she played them a deputation of West Africans appeared on our doorstep complaining about the filthy language she was using. The cymbals were various bits of verdigrised brass perched on copper and chrome piping. She climbed in amongst this potpourri of scrap, and with a confidence born of enthusiasm began hitting things with sticks. She played 'Danny Boy' in five-four time for three hours until the neighbours broke the door down and threatened to shoot her if she didn't shut up. As they came through the door they looked in amazement at the rest of the family as we sat silently staring into the fire, thick cushions lashed over our ears with clothesline and string. It wasn't very long before she abandoned the drums, after she hit a cymbal so hard in the middle of 'I'll Take the A Train' that it flew off its stand and flew across the room like a discus, neatly decapitating the statue of the Infant of Prague that the rent man always thought was a toby jug and knocked his pipe out on.

The drums were taken away on a handcart by a local scrap dealer, and my Gran went to town with the money and came back with a phonofiddle. Not many people have seen a phonofiddle (or a fiddlophone, as they're sometimes called). This is what one looks like –

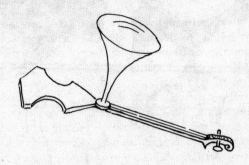

Basically the phonofiddle is a one-string fiddle, but instead of having a pretty body like a violin to amplify the sound it has a horn – such as you get on old wind-up 'His-Master's-Voice'-type gramophones. You play it, held between your knees, with a bow and the resultant sound – as my Grandad once said – is identical to the sound made by a tomcat with its balls caught in a revolving door on a frosty night. After three days of her practising the phonofiddle we took it out of the house by dark of the moon while my Grandmother was fast asleep, and buried it at the bottom of the garden behind the giant Venus' fly-traps she grew for catching pigeons. My Grandfather said a short prayer over it as we stood in the pallid half-light, our breath steamy wisps of vapour.

'And may its pour tormented soul rest in peace,' he muttered, 'and if dat auld biddy digs de bugger up again, I'll wrap it round her bloody neck!'

That afternoon she came home with a guitar, not an ordinary guitar but a national steel guitar, the sort of guitar that was

used by the old negro blues singers out on the Mississippi delta. We stared open-jawed as she took the shining steel thing, fine filigree cut in scrolls all over its front, out of the case and began plucking it with a plectrum, wailing as she did so a blues that in best delta tradition she was making up as she went along.

> *Woke up dis morning, oh Lawdy, got me dem low down blues,*
> *Oh Lawdy, what did I say, I said I woke up dis morning, oh yeah*
> *Lawdy,*
>
> > *Got me dem low down blues,*
> > *Got no shoes on my feet, Lawdy Lawd, got no feet in my shoes,*
> > *Lawdy Lawdy, oh yeah, oh yeah.*

And she played a slow blues riff finishing off with a soulful E-seventh chord.

'Now, Henry,' she cackled gleefully, 'and what do you make of dat?'

'Well,' said my Grandad, 'de music's all right if you like dem kind of tings but if I catch you rubbin' boot polish over yer face you're out of de house!'

'And why would I be doin' dat class of ting at all?'

'Because dem's darky tunes.'

'Be de sacred heart of Jaysus now, would you come out of dat! Did you not know dat de blues comes originally from Oireland?'

'D'ye tell me dat now?'

'I do surely! All dem tunes sung be de class of Howlin' Wolf, Blind Willy MacTell and Sleepy John Estes, was written by de foinest Oirish blues singer dat every laid tonsils on de air dat blows along de Liffey levee – Howlin' Blind Sleepy Liam Patrick O'Shaughnessy.'

'Begob, and dat has everything bate!' said my Grandfather, slapping his thigh which was hanging up on the back of the door.

'Yer man O'Shaughnessy was first cousin to Paul Robeson,' continued my Grandmother.

'Are you telling me dat Paul Robeson was Oirish, now?'

'I am surely. Did yez never hear him singing "Danny boy"?'

'But Paul Robeson was as black as a fireback! Not dat I'm casting nasturtiums on de dark races of de world, yez understand – aren't we all of de wan colour in de sight of de Lord God after all? But you'll not be denyin' me now dat yer man Robeson was as black as midnight in a coal cellar?'

'Dat was on account of de blood pressure and drinkin' too much Guinness,' said my Gran, firmly. 'De whole world knows he had de terrible blood pressure on account of de persecution he received on account of him being a Communist and any but an eejit can see dat if yez drink too much Guinness yez'll end up Guinness-coloured.'

'Begob, and well you learn someting every day,' muttered my Grandfather, staring into the fire as though looking for an explanation there.

'Begob, and you do,' said my Grandmother, 'and here's a song now dat was written be Howlin' Blind Sleepy Liam Patrick O'Shaughnessy,' and she played a two-bar run into a straight twelve-bar blues in E, and with a voice that was cracking the windows screamed out,

Gwine to peel my potatoes,
Peel dem nice and sweet,
Lawdy, Lawdy, Lawdy, gwine to peel my potatoes,
Gwine to peel dem nice and sweet,
Gwine to leave dee eyes in Lawdy, Lawdy,
So dey can see us trew dee week!

She played some flash blues riffs before beginning the second and last verse.

> *Well I'm gwine to gwine*
> *Cos I seed what my man done done,*
> *Oh Lawdy, Lawdy, I'm gwine to gwine*
> *Cos I done seed what my man gwine done done,*
> *Well if he done gwines too*
> *He'll done gwine done what I done gwine done.*

And she finished the song with a fifteen-second display of guitar pyrotechnics and another E-flat seventh chord that tied her fingers up like a ball of wet string.

'Who's dis fella Dunn you're singing about?' muttered my Grandad. 'I knew a Dunn wanst in Castlebar dat ate de insides of a clock and ran off with a nurse to England.'

'What de hell are ye bletherin' on about?' asked my Gran angrily.

'Amn't I telling yer? Ye wuz singing about some feller called Gwine Dunn, well dis fella called Dunn from Castlebar ran off with a nurse to England with de insoides of a clock insoide him.'

'Begob, you're losing yer bloody marbles,' muttered my Grandmother. 'And where are you goin?' she asked, seeing me slinking towards the door.

'I'm going to camp with the Cubs,' I said – this chapter's getting out of hand.

The annual Cub camp took place in Ashworth Valley, a narrow rift in the earth between Manchester and the Pennines proper. It wasn't a real valley at all, so it was said, but had been made by German bombers on their way home dropping all the stuff they'd got left over from redesigning Manchester.

A muddy creek ran at the bottom of a ravine full of sooty shrubs turned black by the fumes from the million factory chimneys that stubbled the landscape below. By night the valley was the favourite haunt of courting couples, who came to find the secrecy and privacy afforded by bushes and grass that would allow them to indulge in the oldest of sports, the making of the two-backed beast, when all you could see in the moonlight was a low-lying mist of steamy breath and a field full of naked men doing press-ups with an extra pair of legs growing out of their backs. The spot was also a favourite with hundreds of families who fled there at weekends and Bank Holidays to come with the children and Gran to picnic and cough. For our campsite we were using a field belonging to a large farm at the head of the valley. There grubby pigs oinked and squealed their days away, and bronchitic chickens huddled under the old railway waggons that were their penthouses and stared out glumly at the rain muttering 'Baawk, buk, buk! Baawk, buk, buk!' which roughly translates as 'God, it's peeing down again! Day after pigging day nothing but pigging rain!'

There was one scrawny-looking sad-eyed old cow and since none of us had ever seen a cow before we came to the conclusion that it was a black and white bus.

'Don't be stupid,' said one of the older Cubs. 'It's a dog with handlebars.'

'It's a big dog,' said Little Weed, one of the smallest Cubs.

'It's got a lot of willies,' said another, pointing to its udders.

Since the field had a cow in it, it naturally also had a fair collection of cow pats. Never having seen things like this before I thought they were stepping stones, and led forty Cubs in follow-my-leader along a line of them across the field. By the time we got to the other side of the field we were both unrecognisable and unbearable, but luckily the constant rain which was a feature of these regions during the period of monsoon quickly washed it all off again and we were soon back to our normal grey colour.

Our Obergruppencubführer was a large lady with legs like

a Wigan prop forward's and bosoms that sailed before her in her Akela's uniform like a green bow wave. One of the cheeky Cubs said he'd once seen Akela's bloomers hanging up on the washing line and they were so big that the man next door had shot holes in them because he said they kept the sun off his radishes. We had laughed at this – not because we believed him but because what he said had been rude.

Once the tents had been erected by Akela and some of the bigger Cubs we did our best to settle down in camp. There were twelve of us to each tent, sleeping six to a side, heads to the walls, feet to the middle. At either end of the tent were doors which laced up at night to keep the smog out. For day after day of that July fortnight the fog rolled down off the moors and, meeting the outfall from the factories of the lowlands, became yellow reeking mist through which a sickly orange sun grinned down for half an hour of each day while the rest of the time acid rain made holes in our green uniforms.

'This is the life, boys!' croaked our Akela. 'The open air, waking up in the morning with the sun on the tent door and running down through the morning dew for a dip in the river…'

'Who's she kidding?' snuffled Wharfie, wringing his cap out before jamming it back on his head and reaching in his pocket for his cough mixture.

One day, when the rain had let up a little and had turned into a mere sullen drizzle, our Akela showed us how to make twists. These were recommended by Baden-Powell in his book *Scouting for Boys* as being nutritious and easy to make. As Billie Holiday might have said, 'Easy you is, nutritious you ain't.' Basically 'twists' consisted of flour and water mixed to the consistency of plasticine which was then rolled into a long worm, wrapped round a stick and held over an open fire until it went grey and hard or – if you were very lucky – a vague crusty bread colour.

101

Dutifully we mixed flour and water on our tin plates and tried to roll it into a ball. Some of the smaller Cubs had put too much water in so that it either ran through their fingers or glued them together so firmly they had to be chiseled apart. Some of us managed to roll ours into vaguely long things though our hands were so grubby that the once-white flour was now the colour of old vests. Round the peeled sticks we wound them, over the fire we held them and when they'd gone hard enough on the outside to make a noise when tapped, we ate them.

Burnt mouths were the order of the day, for beyond the crusted exterior lay a gooey dough the consistency and temperature of molten lava. But, like all small boys, we were constantly hungry and we let neither the temperature nor the texture deter us. As fast as the twists were made they were devoured, until pounds of flour had vanished down the throats of the Cubs like worms into the ever-open beaks of baby sparrows and forty little boys, their bellies swollen and tight lay supine and whimpering, in the warm drizzle.

That night the screams of indigestion and cramp were pitiful. From every tent came groans and wails and the sound of splintering wood as teeth sank into tent poles.

Next morning Akela, with dark circles of sleeplessness round her eyes, knelt before a collection of damp sticks and grass in the drizzle, blowing fiercely on the few dull sparks she had managed to coax out of what was supposed to be our breakfast fire. Above it was slung a dixie containing a bright orange lumpy sludge that was supposed to be baked beans for forty-one.

The fire went from spark to smoke without producing flame, and a thin trail of acrid black murk ascended into the sky as all around stood forty hungry cubs with runny noses and chattering teeth.

Akela stood up, red-faced and breathless, her uniform

hanging on her like wet sodden camouflage round a tank. 'Get me the paraffin,' she whimpered hoarsely. We watched as she swung the can of paraffin backwards and forwards, carefully taking aim.

'One!' she cried.

'Two!' we chorused.

'Three!' we all yelled, and seven-eighths of a gallon of paraffin landed in the dixie full of beans, the remaining eighth landing on the fire and causing it to sputter half-heartedly into life. Our six were supposed to be doing the cooking that morning, and so we were close enough to the fire to have seen what had happened. The rest of the Cubs had wandered downwind of the fire, hoping to catch a whiff of the smell of cooking food.

We scooped as much of the paraffin off as we could, but there was still a good quarter-inch thick skin of paraffin oil remaining at the end of it all.

'What do we do now?' I asked Wharfie.

'We stir it in,' he said out of the corner of his mouth. 'We'll be here all bloody day if we have to get it all out.' So with the biggest spoon available we turned the beans and paraffin into an emulsion, a dish of novel cuisine which Wharfie christened and wrote on the menu blackboard as '*Haricot à l'huile de lampe*', he being the only one to speak fluent French and therefore the only one able to understand it.

The hungry Cubs lined up, plates at the ready. One after the other they received their large dollops of beans and slices of bread and marge and from all over the rainy field came cries of 'These beans taste funny' and 'Yeah, but I'm still eating them. I'm starving, me!'

That night the campsite was like Piccadilly Circus. There were Cubs with the squitters passing Cubs with the trots bumping into Cubs with the Delhi belly. The Aztec two-step had taken over the entire camp – with the exception of our six, who had left the beans severely alone and who lay snug and smug in our sleeping bags. The night air was rent asunder with noises and moans. Two Cubs passing each other close to our tent had the following hurried conversation:

Cub One: 'How many times have you been? I've been sixty-seven times already.'

Cub Two: 'Ninety-three, me! Me bum's like a cherry!'

The last bits of paper were used, even to the greaseproof wrapping from the sliced bread. Dock leaves were at a premium and were changing hands for marbles and Dinky toys. In desperation, one Cub used stinging nettles and beat the world record for the hop, skip and jump by ten yards.

In the morning light the Cubs looked like the survivors of a Japanese death camp, and the air was thick with mutiny.

A deputation from the pack came to our tent. 'This place is going to kill us,' said one.

'We want to go home,' said another.

'I want my mum!' said he of the hop, skip and jump.

'There's only one way we're going to get out of this alive,' I said, my training as an anarchist coming to the fore. 'We've got to stage a coup.'

'A Scottish cow?' asked one of the Cubs.

'No, a coup,' I said.

'How do you spell that?' asked Hop, Skip and Jump.

'C O U P – the 'p' is silent like the 'p' in bath.'

'That's stupid,' said Hop, Skip and Jump. 'That would mean that stoop is stoo, rope is roe and pope is poe?'

I raised my hand authoritatively. 'This is no time to discuss semantics, brothers. We've got to topple this regime and replace it with a democratically-elected saviour and son of the people.'

'Who's that?' asked Hop, Skip and Jump.

'Wharfie,' I replied, figuring out in true politician's fashion that if the coup failed it would be Wharfie's neck that would be on the block. If it succeeded then I could lead a simple counter-coup that would remove him from power. I could then discredit him, have his head taken off all the stamps and money and have all his statues demolished.

Word spread round the camp that Wharfie was bidding to take over as Akela. The plan was simple. In the night, blacked up, several of the bigger Cubs would sneak into Akela's tent, overpower her and gag and bind her. We would then dip into her purse and take out enough money for forty bus fares home.

'And for forty ice lollies,' said Wharfie. 'Why should the ruling cadre be the only ones to know the pleasures of decadence?'

The coup failed.

Quite simply, we hadn't reckoned on one of our number's sneaking, nor had we ever taken into account Akela's prodigious strength. She was ready and waiting in her tent when the platoon went into action. The first Cub went in with face blackened and a balaclava pulled over his head. There was a roar, a smacking noise and one after the other Cubs in various stages of unconsciousness exploded through the tent door and landed on the wet grass.

'I want my mum,' cried Hop, Skip and Jump, his words muffled by a mouthful of nettles.

In the next field to us were a troop of Boy Scouts. They were from one of the posher areas of town and had proper uniforms and equipment – unlike ours, which looked as though it had come from the Visigoth Army Surplus Stores. They tried to bully us on the first day of camp, but soon changed their tactics when one of our Cubs (who was in fact thirty-six but small for his age) was picked on by a big Scout from their Peewit Patrol. Our Cub tore the Scout's arm off and then made him ask for it back.

The Scoutmaster and our Akela, however, seemed to develop an instant rapport. We could hardly get breakfast cooked some days for these two making sheep's eyes at each other across the drystone-wall that divided the Cubs' camp from the Scouts' camp. On several occasions our sixer had to go to Akela and pull on her skirt, pointing out that the beans were on fire or that the bacon was now like shoelaces and the eggs like puncture patches.

One night we heard noises coming from Akela's tent. Glasses and bottles clinked and there was the sound of muffled laughter and merriment.

'They're going to make babies,' nodded Wharfie sagely.

'How do they do that?' I asked innocently (you must remember that in those days children were much less well informed about matters sexual, and in fact I did not find out about the facts of life until Chapter 7).

106

Now Wharfie, who was a little more worldly-wise than us, had seen drawings in the toilets in town and in the cinema that had given him a crude – if incomplete – visual understanding of the processes of human reproduction. The most explicit drawing he had seen had been executed by someone with an IQ slightly above that of a gherkin and was so badly drawn that the female organ looked like an ear, while the male organ looked like an index finger jutting from a bunched fist, rather like those Victorian direction signs you still sometimes see.

'I'll tell you how they're going to make a baby,' said Wharfie importantly. 'He's going to stick his finger in her ear,' and he said it with such authority that we believed him completely.

We listened attentively as the sounds grew louder and more urgent. We heard the rustle of clothes, the popping of press studs, the zipping of zippers and the twanging of elastic.

'What are they doing now?' I asked.

'I think they're making a dress,' muttered Wharfie. There was a brief gasp, then the sound of flesh on rubber that I now realise was the noise of Akela getting on to the lilo. I also realise, looking back, that Akela weighing in at twenty-four stone or so, and the Scoutmaster tipping the scales at another thirteen or fourteen, meant that a total of some thirty-seven or more stone were pummelling what is, after all, nothing more than a large segmented balloon.

There was a groan and a whimper, then silence followed by a cry of 'Oh, oh! Oh, Ronald! Oh Ronald! It's nice, but it's hurting.'

'She must have wax in her ears,' said Little Weed.

The noises of flesh on inflated rubber grew louder and more frantic.

'They're hitting each other,' said Weed.

'No, they're playing snap,' said Wharfie.

A hoarse voice cried, 'Oh my God, oh my God, you're so good for me.'

107

'They're praying together,' I said. 'He must be a Catholic too.'

The voice of our Akela shouted out, 'I'm coming! I'm coming!' followed almost immediately by the voice of the Scoutmaster shouting, 'So am I, so am I.'

'That's funny,' said Wharfie, 'I thought they were already there. How can you be coming from somewhere when you're both in a tent?'

'Oh, oh, oh! I'm going to die! I'm going to die!' screamed our Akela.

'He's killing her!' I shouted. 'Quick, Wharfie, we've got to save her! Get me your airgun!'

Wharfie had brought his Diana air pistol to camp with him. I took aim with it and fired it towards our Akela's tent. There was a popping sound, then silence for a brief few seconds then – with a violent hissing roar – the lilo, with Akela and the Scoutmaster still aboard, burst the door asunder and shot out

of the tent, jet-propelled, flying across the field with our Akela screaming, 'This is the best ever! Ever!'

The lilo hit a barbed-wire fence and exploded, catapulting the two lovers down the valley side into the brook, locked together like Ahab on the great white whale.

'Do you think we'll understand these things when we grow up?' I asked Wharfie.

'I'm not sure I want to understand them,' he muttered.

6

God's Own Drunk

When I became an altar boy, my Grandmother's joy verged on ecstasy. 'Begob, and isn't havin' an altar boy in de family de next best ting to havin' a priest in de family?' And she shoved a pinch of snuff up her nose that would have killed a carthorse.

I don't know whether she thought my being an altar boy might mean that she got extra helpings at Communion or lighter penances at Confession, but my own reasons for being an altar boy were partly mystical and one hundred per cent mercenary. The severe white surplice trimmed with lace over the high buttoned black cassock brought you kudos with relatives, a certain amount of pulling power with girls (if you were interested in that kind of thing, which I wasn't at the time), and also virtually guaranteed you a steady supply of half-crowns and ten-bob notes from happy relatives at weddings when you served Nuptial Mass and from distraught or drunk relatives at Requiems.

The mysticism is more difficult to understand. There was no calling from above, no blinding flash on the road to Tarsus, no still small voice crying to me from far into the night, just the realisation that if I had to go to church every Sunday I might as well get paid for doing so. There was very little in the way of anything religious in my make-up, really, since I'd discovered quite young that religion generally got me into trouble.

In my first days at school Miss Worswick had said, 'Now, children, we all have something deep inside us that is the most important part of us. Does anybody know what this little part of us is? We've all got this little part but you can't see it no matter how hard we try.' I heard Michael Coffee next to me mutter, 'Our souls' out of the side of his mouth. The problem was that in Manchester the word 'our' is very often pronounced 'are' – as in 'ar' kid and 'ar' 'ouse'. These figures of speech are further complicated by 'our' meaning 'my', so that 'ar' kid' means 'my brother' and 'ar' ouse' means 'my house'. The real problem on this occasion was that 'our souls' coming from the mouth of Coffee – he of the green candles on the upper lip – sounded like 'ar' souls'; which seemed to me to be the perfect answer to the clue 'you can't see it no matter how hard you try'. After all, put your hands up all those who, without the aid of mirror or Polaroid camera, can honestly say that they've seen their own arseholes?

My hand shot up. 'I know, Miss Worswick.'

'Oh very good, Michael, and what's the answer?'

'Arseholes, Miss Worswick.'

The world fell in, lights exploded in my ears and bells went off before my eyes.

When in a further religious lesson I volunteered the information that the patron saint of children was Noddy, and the patron saint of animals was Tarzan, my reputation as a fool and suspect pagan was firmly established.

When she found out I was going to be an altar boy, Miss Worswick told Monsignor McGuinness to count the candlesticks.

'Sure, the lad's as honest as the days are long,' he told her.

'It's the middle of winter, it doesn't get light until nine o'clock and goes dark again at four,' she reminded him.

Monsignor McGuinness counted the candlesticks.

The business side of being an altar boy was easy – at least for me it was. I learnt all the responses I had to make in Latin, learnt how to ring the bells, pour the wine and water and hold the communion plate at Mass and how to swing the thurifer, a metal ball on chains with burning incense inside, at Benediction. When I served my first Mass the whole family came. It was nine o'clock in the morning and it being a lovely summer's morning the church was packed to the rafters with keen Catholic golfers and fervent Catholic fishermen who wanted to get Mass over early. In the front rows, jammed in like peas in a pod, were the usual dozen or so religious lunatics who went to every Mass, Benediction, wedding, Stations of the Cross and funeral there was. They spent so much time in church they had got squatters' rights on it, and so much time on their knees that a pair of shoes would last them ten years and only ever wore out at the toes.

Into this army of the ungodly and the unhinged came my Grandmother and Grandfather, my Mother and Molly, the Monsignor's housekeeper. My Grandmother away from her hearing aid not only didn't hear well, but spoke all the time in a loud shout like a demented newspaper seller. She came into church and, for all the world as though she was hawking the *Manchester Evening News* on the corner of Market Street in a thunderstorm, screamed, 'SACRED HEART OF JAYSUS! YOU'D THINK THEY'D GIVE THE STATUES A LICK OF PAINT. DE VIRGIN MARY'S NOSE DERE IS FLAKIN' LIKE A CHRYSANTHEMUM AND ST JOSEPH IS SO SOOTY HE

LOOKS LIKE SUGAR RAY ROBINSON.'

She looked around her breathing heavily down her nose. 'DAT AULD BUGGER MCGUINNESS GOES SWANNIN' ABOUT IN A NEW CAR EVERY YEAR AND DE NOSE IS FALLIN' OFF DE MOTHER OF GOD FOR DE WANT OF A COAT OF PAINT! BEGOB I'LL BUY A TIN OF GLOSS PINK MESELF FROM WOOLIES AND SHAME DE OLD BUGGER.'

When I walked on to the altar behind Monsignor McGuinness I heard my Grandmother's voice ringing round the church. 'LOVE OF GOD, DERE HE IS AND LOOK AT HIM. IF HE HAD WINGS HE'D BE AN ANGEL.'

'Would you come on out of dat now. You're showin' me up,' said my Grandad, 'and give a man some room on de kneeler dere. I've got one leg in de aisle.'

But my Grandmother, deaf to his every syllable, carried on as though she were talking to somebody back home in Dublin without the benefit of a phone.

'DEAR GOD, AND ISN'T IT A WONDERFUL TING DAT A CHOILD SO YOUNG SHOULD BE SERVING GOD ON DE ALTAR. DE CHOILD'S A GENIUS, SO HE IS.'

From all around the church the noise of hushing and shushing came, the religious fanatics were glaring over their shoulders at my Grandmother who snorted back at them down her nose, while the fishermen and golfers were earnestly praying that McGuinness would not stop the show and hold Mass up while he threw the old lunatic out, making them late in the locker room or on the canal bank.

Serving with me that morning was a boy called O'Hara. O'Hara was from a long line of religious fanatics. Half the craw-thumpers and holy water addicts there that morning were blood relatives of his. He had a terrible squint, so that when he spoke to you you always looked around just in case there was somebody else there he was really talking to, and he had a face so covered with boils it looked like a map of the

114

moon. He was two years older than me and it was his responsibility that morning to ring the bells for the offertory when the priest offers the bread and wine for consecration. As he rang the bell, I stood up and moved to take my place at the side of the altar. I caught my foot in my cassock as I rose and tumbled over in a heap.

'BEGOB DAT SQUINT-EYED BUGGER WID DE BELL'S LEGGED 'IM UP!' howled my Grandmother, banging her fist on the pew. The massed lunatics glared at her, a sea of popping eyes. I stood at the side of the altar with the wine and water. Monsignor McGuinness came over to me with the chalice. Out of the side of his mouth he muttered. 'If the old fool doesn't shut up, old lady or not I'll throw her down the steps meself.'

I nodded, and poured a little wine. Just as I was taking the wine away he tapped the wine jug. I looked at him. He nodded. I poured some more wine, looked up at him, and he nodded again. I poured even more wine and was about to move the wine jug away when he tapped it once again with the chalice. I looked up, he nodded. I poured some more wine. By now the jug was almost empty. He nodded again and I poured the last dregs into the chalice. I brought the water jug over towards the chalice and had poured three drops into the chalice when he tapped the water jug urgently. I looked at him and he shook his head slightly. So he didn't like a little water with his wine but believed, as St Paul said, that we should all take a little wine for our stomach's sake. In his case he was taking it for his stomach, his liver, his kidneys and at least one of his legs. He moved back to the middle of the altar and drank it in one go.

When it came to the Communion I carried the communion plate before him, holding it under the chins of the recipients as they, eyes closed and tongues out, waited for the body of God to be placed firmly on their tongues. As we approached my Grandmother I dropped a stick of chewing gum on to the plate. McGuinness looked down. He was known to have terrible eyesight and was now half-drunk anyway so that, thinking it to be a host that he'd inadvertently dropped (hosts did in fact sometimes stick together hence the communion plate was held under the chalice and the chin of the recipient) he pressed the chewing gum onto my Grandmother's tongue. We carried on down the row giving Communion to the rest of the congregation until the last of the lunatics, fishermen and golfers had walked back to their places, hands together and eyes looking earnestly down at the floor. As I turned to walk back up the altar I noticed my Grandmother – her face contorted and twisted with effort, her top and bottom set firmly glued together with Wrigley's spearmint gum, no sounds coming out but snuffles and muffled grunts that sounded like unborn shouts and curses.

Every year on the feast day of Our Lady our church held a procession at which one of the little girls crowned the statue of the Virgin with a wreath of artificial flowers as the rest of us sang hymns and did other quasi-religious things. In fact, the processions never left the grounds of the church or school; we merely perambulated round a route of a hundred yards or so, circling the lawn where we ran our egg and spoon races on sports' day, trailing past the heap of coke destined for the boilers and, continuing down by the bike shed, turned into church. So short was the route that on one occasion the tail of the procession was caught by the head and, like a caucus race, the whole string of parishioners went round and round the circuit until those of a more nervous disposition got dizzy and fell over. My Gran said that the reason we never left the grounds was that the Protestants would stone us. I knew that that wasn't true, and that the real reason was that we didn't want the Protestants to see how poorly dressed we were.

One year I was in the team of altar boys carrying crosses, bells and thurifers at the head of the procession. It was a hot sunny afternoon and parents were crying emotionally at the sight of the twelve-year-old girl who was to crown the Virgin. Bernadette McClusky, who by now had cornered the world market in jelly babies, was clad in white satin and lace. Her face was serene and beatific, her gaze calm and worshipful, the overall effect one of virginal purity – broken only for a brief second when she winked at one of the thurifer swingers as we came by the bike shed with a wink so suggestive that, as he swung it, his thurifer flew out of his hand and vanished with a following tail of smoke over the roof of the infants' classroom.

'Mother of God, it's a comet!' My Gran blessed herself.

The catastrophe occurred near the church. A swarm of bees were busily working amongst the flowers of the herbaceous border fringing the unhealthy lawn beside our concrete playground. The sole function of the lawn was to be looked at, the sole function of the playground was for us to fall down and hurt ourselves. If this seems perverse to you, then I can only say that it makes sense to a Catholic – remember it was a nun who invented barbed wire.

As we walked past the bees, several of them – attracted by the scarlet of the Monsignor's garb – detached themselves from the scavengers amongst the flora and began to circle him. Now it was customary in those processions for the Monsignor to stop, every so often, turn round and bless us at which time the whole procession would halt and kneel as he made the sign of the cross in the air above our heads. He would then signal for us to rise by extending both arms and bringing them towards him palm upwards then, with a sideways motion of his left hand, he would cue the choir who would begin the next hymn as we processed churchwards.

One of the circling bees landed on his nose. He turned in fright and tried to brush it away. Five hundred people fell to their knees. He tried to knock it to one side and the choir started singing. He hit out at two more bees to the left and right of him and everybody stood up. He made a lunge at a bee in front of his face and half the congregation knelt, the other half crossed themselves, started walking forward and fell over those who were still kneeling. His movements grew more frantic and uncoordinated. The choir, thinking he was telling them to hurry up, began singing faster and faster until the words ran together and several of them fell down breathless. The fitter among the congregation were jumping up and down from a kneeling to a standing position and back again like a mass practising of the Canadian Air force exercises. A particularly violent swinging motion on the Monsignor's behalf got the thurifer swingers following suit, their thurifers spinning above the crowd, sending sparks over the heads of the furthest and intoxicating the nearest with their fumes, so that they began hallucinating, wailing and singing and

pointing at things they could see in the empty air. Still he flapped at the bees, still people jumped up and down and fell over each other.

'Make your bloody mind up, McGuinness!' shouted my Grandmother as, with a new wave of his arms, half the congregation prostrated itself on the ground facing Mecca, the rest of them started dancing the okey cokey and the altar boys, under the baleful eyes of McGuinness, lay on the ground helpless with laughter.

My life as an altar boy was not a long one, my dismissal from the service not obligatory but compulsory; the reason for my dismissal twofold – the incident with the altar wine and the altar boys' strike. I'll deal with them in reverse order.

I've always been a firm believer in unions, in spite of their many faults, since it has been my experience that if you give a boss an inch he'll take several miles and ask you: (a) to do it in your own time, and (b) to supply your own tools.

It's also my opinion that if employers found out that their workers could live on a diet of fresh air then most bosses would ask not only if they could work harder but also if they could breathe less while they were doing so. It's always struck me as strange that what the public applaud in bosses (i.e. the profit motive) is called unpatriotic in workers; and whereas the boss holding the threat of the sack over their heads is called 'responding to market forces', workers threatening to strike are called 'disruptive, anarchistic, communistic and anti-democratic', when like the bosses the workers are simply asking for more for less. As my Grandad used to say 'if arseholes were solid gold only the rich would have them'.

The strike of the altar boys began over both wages and conditions. On almost every occasion, the tips from weddings and funerals were paid directly to the altar boys on the one hand and to the choirboys on the other. We then divided it up amongst ourselves in a fairly equal ratio. McGuinness one day made a policy statement whereby all monies were to be paid directly to him. We were to tell anybody who offered us a tip after a wedding or a funeral that they were please to give it to Monsignor McGuinness, who would then divide it up equally amongst the choirboys and the altar boys. After a few weeks of this regime it became clear that McGuinness was taking a big rake-off as our average gross takings dropped from pounds to pence. There was a hurried meeting of choir- and altar boys in Lorenzini's milk bar, where the problem of wages was discussed along with the general problem of conditions. The conditions were in fact terrible. Badly-fitting cassocks (I myself had a cassock that had been taken up and down so many times it looked like a concertina), cheap incense that made you cough, cheap candles that burnt so fast that the scalding hot wax ran down on to your fingers and, worst of all, the Monsignor's dog.

The Monsignor had an albino Jack Russell terrier that in human years would have been around two hundred years old. It lay in front of the one-bar electric fire that was switched on in the vestry winter and summer, smelling of warm dog, decay and rot in summer, and of wet dog, decay and rot in winter. Like the Monsignor himself it had to all intents and purposes remained celibate. Unlike the Monsignor it relieved its sexual frustrations by rogering small boys' legs.

Cross-eyed and panting it would cling to your leg like a crazed sloth, its stubby paws welded around your calf, its little pink willy caught in the elastic of your sock. If the Monsignor saw the dog so pleasuring itself he would cry, 'Now, Brutus, that's naughty. Stop it.' And the dog took as much notice as fly to the moon, rattling on like an erotic grinning cocktail shaker. Molloy had cured it for a while by smearing Sloane's liniment on his leg. The dog grabbed him, began stage one – and then ran howling round the church, licking himself. Every lick burnt his tongue and made him jump and howl the more, so that like a perpetual motion machine he kept up a frantic wailing, running, jumping and licking motion for nearly three hours.

In a unanimous vote, the result of which was later toasted in sarsaparilla, it was decided that I should be the one who presented our case to Monsignor McGuinness. When I told him in the sacristy after eleven o'clock Mass on Sunday he looked at me with eyes like currants in a teacake and muttered through tight lips, 'Go and open the door.' When I'd done that, he snarled 'Stand there'.

I stood looking out at the world outside as, with a technique born of ten years of Gaelic football, he drop-kicked me down the steps and across the lawn. That night, at Benediction, we struck. A total withdrawal of labour was not possible because O'Hare and the head altar boy Dillon scabbed. We formed picket lines and burnt old hymn books to keep warm. To keep our spirits up we sang revolutionary songs like 'Viva la quinza

Brigada', the 'Red Army Marching Song', and 'The Man Who Waters the Workers' Beer' while to annoy the people going into Confession we sang 'Three German Officers Crossed the Line' and 'She Was Poor But She Was Honest'.

For three months we held out as Dillon and O'Hare got fat on our pickings, and even received a bonus for signing a no-strike agreement. Feelings round the parish were deeply divided; there were some who said we should have had a ballot but we replied that we'd already balloted with our feet. Many of the parishioners supported us, others said it was sinful to withdraw our labour in this way. Some Jewish cantors from the local synagogue sent fraternal greetings and pledges of support together with a parcel of lox and bagels and a yamulka for every striker embroidered with mottoes such as: 'The wages of sin are death, The wages of grace are pitiful!', 'Remember 1926', and 'Altar boys do it for peanuts'.

Some Church of England choirboys joined the picket lines one Sunday morning and there was a nasty incident when one of them hit O'Hare with a flower pot. There was a mêlée which the local press reported as intimidation and the following Sunday the scabs were bused into Mass in Morris Minors by a gang of Empire Loyalists and local Tories. The next Sunday after that, our numbers swelled by the remains of the Mystery Riders anarcho-syndicalists and theirs swelled by members of the local Boys Brigade, a running battle took place which resulted in broken front teeth, black eyes all round and the cancellation of eleven o'clock Mass and Benediction that morning.

McGuinness gave interviews to the local press, accusing us of intimidating our members and being undemocratic and, true to form, the press was on his side. One photographer spent all his time camped outside our house trying to take photographs of me that made me look as though I was wearing a wig. When I waved at a friend across the street I was photographed and the picture of me with arm upraised was shown in the *Crumpsall Comet* captioned, 'Heil Harding!!! Who does he think he is?'

The strike was finally broken when news reached Rome, and the Pope sent a platoon of papal guards to make sure that the scabs got through and to intimidate or bribe the rest of us back to work with Hornby 'double-O' train sets, which they said had been blessed by the Pope himself. In the face of such opposition, a hostile press and limited resources, morale dropped, the strike crumbled and after three months – beaten but not broken, and wiser after the event – we returned to our duties. McGuinness peered over the chalice that morning with a look that told me my card was marked.

After the incident with the altar wine my career as an altar boy was over and my reputation as a drunk, unearned as it was, established. The altar wine was kept in a large cupboard in the vestry and only Monsignor McGuinness and the other two priests, Father O'Driscoll and Father Zborgwensky, had keys. Another altar boy, Boylan, who had already got a taste for the booze by wheedling invitations to wedding receptions after Nuptial Mass, took an impression of the key one day in a cake of soap and made a duplicate key in metalwork class at school. At first we merely took a sip from the great glass jar in the cupboard that smelt of beeswax but gradually, emboldened by that one sip, we took larger and larger swigs until we would often present ourselves for inspection just before Mass reeling and giddy and reeking of drink. McGuinness knew that somebody was having the wine away but suspected the other two priests rather than the boys since the priests had keys. O'Driscoll, in particular, with his known habit of falling down in the Catholic club after closing time suffering from liquor mortis, was a prime suspect.

'Do you think that Father O'Driscoll does go a little heavy on the wine?' McGuinness asked Boylan one day.

'He does seem to like us to fill the chalice right up to the top, Monsignor,' replied Boylan, trying to keep a look of innocence in his red-rimmed eyes and hiding his shaking hands inside his trouser pockets.

McGuinness just nodded and swept out with a swirl of his red cassock like Zorro looking for his horse.

A new carboy of wine and Christmas Eve were our undoing. We arrived at church late on Christmas Eve to get ready for Midnight Mass. This is the most important event, in a way, in the whole liturgical calendar since it is the Mass at which the rebirth of hope into the world is celebrated and the new year really begins. It was at this Mass also that red-eyed and weeping, legions of drunks swayed in rows at the back of the church like bierfest celebrants in a Munich bierhalle, vowing repentance, grace and goodness for the rest of their days.

Boylan and I found the vestry empty and, on opening the cupboard, we discovered a brand new carboy of wine stood there, deeper amber than any we had seen previously and when we filled the jug fumes that had our eyes watering filled the room. We poured a paper cupful each.

'Happy Christmas' we wished each other, knocking the cupful back in one as was our wont. Immediately the world changed colour and the glowing ball that was my stomach began to float out of position and wander round my body until it settled somewhere between my ears.

'Bloody hell fire,' gasped Boylan, his face swelling and writhing before my eyes like a speeded-up film of rising dough.

Had we but known it, the vintner who bottled the wine had accidentally bottled kosher rum in mistake for altar wine – which rum was roughly a hundred and ten per cent proof and should really only have been used for lighting fires, preserving wooden legs and as an additive in high explosives.

After another cupful apiece we were in no pain at all, and set the altar for Mass as though in a dream. In a haze we stood before McGuinness for inspection and followed him out of the vestry on to the altar like sleepwalkers.

To the words 'Dominus vobiscum' (which means 'The Lord go with you') we were supposed to answer 'Et cum spiritu tui' – ('and with your spirit').

'Dominus vobiscum,' intoned McGuinness.

'You too,' muttered Boylan, falling over. Almost immediately he got up again and shouted, 'There's a crocodile on the altar.' The congregation, who were largely drunk, got jammed in the aisles trying to escape from the crocodile. Seventeen of them claimed that they could see it too, while another thirty claimed it was not a crocodile in fact but a bright yellow giraffe with fangs and a machine gun. By the time McGuinness got the congregation back in their seats Boylan was standing in the pulpit singing.

> *She wears red feathers and a hula-hula skirt,*
> *She wear red feathers and a hula-hula skirt,*
> *She lives on just coconuts*
> *And fish from the sea.*

Some of the congregation had begun to join in when Boylan whooped like a Red Indian and fell from sight inside the pulpit.

In the mean time I'd remained in a kneeling position at the foot of the altar convinced, firstly, that I was paralysed and, secondly, that the carpet on the altar was in fact grass and that it was full of snakes. Boylan climbed out of the pulpit and fell on his head. I went behind the organ and was violently and noisily sick on to three younger members of the choir who had been having a smoke behind the pipes. Two replacement altar boys were brought in and Boylan and I were sent home in disgrace, never to serve again.

It was my first experience of being drunk and in the morning came my first hangover. Men with pneumatic drills were working inside my head while a controlled series of nuclear explosions were taking place in the space just above my eyes. I sat at the breakfast table staring at my runny eggs and bacon, unable even to lift my fork, my tongue stuck to the roof of my mouth like a dead mouse.

'De ungrateful auld bugger,' said my Gran when I told her that I'd been sacked from the job (omitting, of course, to tell her the reason why), 'after all the hard work yous did for McGuinness. Dere's many a time I've seen yer fallin' down trew dis door dead beat.'

'Dead drunk', I thought, would have been a fitter description.

If You Do That, You'll Go Blind And All Your Children Will Be Born Thin

If you were eleven years old in 1956 sex was another country and you hadn't even got a passport, never mind the plane fare. In a world composed of images culled from *Just William*, *Treasure Island*, The Three Stooges, Bugs Bunny, Popeye, *Biggles* and Dan Dare, the processes of reproduction weren't even hinted at, never mind mentioned. Bodies were things to be shot, stabbed, punched, zoomed into space, beaten into submission in the mines of the Mekon and made to perform incredible feats at the hands of cartoonists. They were never to be seen naked and certainly not in bed together. Women in this hotch-potch of literature that formed the horizons of my world were either mothers, in which case they inhabited some region reserved for gods or superhuman beings, or they were sisters, aunts and cousins, that vague band of beings who either told tales on you, giggled or gave you advice.

Grandmothers belonged to a time when dinosaurs roamed

the earth and the wheel was a vague idea gathering dust at the back of a drawer in the Lascaux patents office. They were not flesh and blood like other mortals, but were rather like those machines you used to find at the seaside that – when fed with a penny – came to life as a haunted house with ghosts and skeletons flitting in and out of cupboards or an execution scene with hangman and gallows.

Girls our own age existed as things simply to be teased or shouted after in the street. We boys didn't take them seriously, stupidly all the time thinking we were braver and brighter than they were and not knowing in fact that it was the other way round, and that it was us boys that were the weaker and dafter sex. But when you're eleven such ideas are light-years away. Life is still a great mystery, run largely on cartoon principles. Goodies and baddies exist in a world that seems truly black and white, and when you shoot people they don't really drop down in a sad mangled heap, they argue with you about who shot first, who is really dead and if they lose the argument they take their ball and go home. If only real war was like that.

If you were an eleven-year-old boy in 1956, your body was something that helped you climb trees and ride a bike, and anything else was a total and absolute mystery. All I knew about my body was that there was something vaguely shifty or unmentionable about the area between navel and knee (or, in my Grandmother's case, between chin and ankle). I remember that we got a clockwork television in 1956. My Grandfather, who had bought it off a man in a pub, proudly brought it in and set it on the table. When he had wound it up, we all sat round to watch 'Sunday Night at the London Palladium'. The first act to take the stage were the Tiller Girls, a long-legged set of lasses whose act was composed basically of dance routines in which, wearing little tunics, little feathers and little else, they kicked long fishnet-clad legs high into the air. They'd hardly kicked twice before my Grandmother's steel guitar crashed through the screen of the television and she wailed, 'De brazen hussies! Would yous look at dat now! What in God's name do they tink dey're doin' showin' such a class of filth in a Catlick household?'

When she heard that the same picture would be seen all over England she almost died. 'Begob. D'ye tell me dat now!' she shrieked as she emptied a bottle of holy water over the wreckage. 'You mean dere could be priests and nuns watching dat self-same film-um we just seed?'

'I do surely,' said my Grandfather, sweeping up the bits.

'Well I hope to God deir housekeepers have enough common sense to take hammers and smash de filthy yokes up. Television is it! Begod, if Auld Nick himself had come walkin' out of it I wouldn't have been surprised!'

I was vaguely aware that there was something wrong, or if not wrong then decidedly strange, about that region of our bodies known to include 'de mickey' but I would no more have linked it with having babies than believe that Dan Dare wore dresses in the privacy of his bedroom at Space College. Babies were a total mystery to me. I remember one day my Uncle Bernard was reading the tablecloth, my Grandfather sat skrimshawing in the corner, my Uncle Harry was still looking for a machine that would make him into a millionaire and I was sitting in a chair, thinking. Uncle Bernard looked up from the tablecloth and said, 'It says here that British troops have gone into the Suez Canal.'

'Begob,' cried my Grandmother, 'I knew that if dey didn't fence it in someone would fall in one of dese days! I've no love for de British Army, dem havin' taken me husband and me two sons to war but I wouldn't wish dem any harm and God knows dey're all mudder's sons. Was dere anyone drownded at all?'

'It's in de Suez,' said Uncle Bernard, cranking the hearing aid.

'God save us, dat's even worse. I wouldn't want any son of mine splashing round in dat class of stuff. What de hell was de Army doing in de sewers in the first place?'

Uncle Bernard just shrugged his shoulders and gave up.

'Gran,' I asked, 'where do babies come from?'

There was a brief cold silence. Then my Grandad spat a mouthful of hot tea into the fire and fell against the canoe, coughing and choking. Uncle Bernard hid his head in the tablecloth and my Grandmother looked at me with eyes like tin baths full of treacle.

'I'll wash yer mouth out with soap,' she scolded. 'Did yez hear dat, Molly?' she asked her cousin the housekeeper.

'Begob and I did, Mary Ellen,' said Molly, who was sitting by the fire reading a Catholic Truth Society pamphlet entitled *I Was A Methodist Burglar*. 'You'd wonder where de young people of today are going to end up at all. Begob, dey'd break dere mudders' hearts, so they would, wid deir questions.'

'Choild o'grace!' said my Grandmother. 'Whatever put ideas like dat into yer head?'

'Well,' I said, 'I saw a lady pushing a pram today and there was a baby in it. And I know where prams come from cos I've seen them in the same shop that you buy bikes from but I don't know where you get babies from. Wharfie said that a man and a lady can get a baby if the man puts his whatsisname —'

'Sacred heart of Jaysus! Would you stop now before you have de roof fallin' in on us all!' said my Gran, whirling her rosary round her head.

'. . . his finger in her ear,' I finished lamely.

'His finger in her ear! Is dat what dem street arabs you go running about wid told yez? Dat's all me eye and Peggy Martin. Babies only come when men and women are married and pray very hard for a baby and Almighty God if he sees fit send dem wan down.'

'Well, Wharfie says it's something to do with belly buttons.'

'Not at all,' snorted my Grandad. 'De belly button is for de convenience of de dark tribes of Africa who don't have de luxury of beds as we do over here. When yer man in de Congo gets tired he cuts a stick off a tree and pokes it in his belly button and turns himself into a tripod. Dat way he can sleep standin' up widdout de ants gettin' into his loin cloth, and if de lions and tigers or polar bears come trew de jungle he's in a good startin' position to run away from dem and climb a tree.'

'But why have we all got belly buttons? We don't live in the jungle?'

'Ah now,' said my Grandad, tapping the side of his nose with his scrimshaw knife, 'dat's because God is powerful clever. Point one, if he makes us all de same it means he only has to have de wan mould, and point two, it means if yez ever go to Africa ye'll have somewhere to poke yer sleeping stick. Udderwise ye'd be falling off all night.'

This answer didn't satisfy me and, still puzzled about where babies came from, I embarked on a systematic programme of research. We'd done projects at school on cocoa and tea and I remembered that our teacher had told us that if we went to the library we would be able to find out everything we wanted to know from books.

At the library the next day the librarian refused to tell me where the books on where babies come from were kept. 'You're a dirty-minded little tyke,' she screamed, hitting me over the head with a copy of *Zen and the Poultry Farmer*.

'We've drawn another blank,' I told Wharfie, who was waiting outside the library. 'We're never going to find out.'

'I think it's something to do with having no clothes on,' said Wharfie, 'cos one of the big kids at school said his big sister and her boyfriend took their clothes off one night cos he saw them through the window.'

'Do you mean he took all his clothes off and was bare, totally bare?'

'Yes.'

'And he let her see his mickey?'

'Well, she had no clothes on as well.'

'That's terrible!'

'Then,' said Wharfie, 'she had a baby after that.'

'Straight away?'

'No, you have to wait a long time, nearly a year. But you can put your clothes back on while you wait.'

We had consulted *Scouting for Boys*, our Bible in those days, but the only advice it contained was something about a chap not having anything to do with a girl he wouldn't want his mother or sister to see him with, and another bit about not changing your underpants. 'If you are unable,' it said, 'to change your underpants at least once a month then, standing clear of magnetic instruments, remove the underpants, lay them on a flat piece of ground and beat them with a stick until they no longer make a noise.'

Slowly the realisation that there was a whole world of experience tied up with people taking their clothes off together, and that this world was somehow rude and forbidden yet exciting began to permeate the mass consciousness of our group of eleven-year-olds. One day Wharfie turned up with a picture he'd ripped from an art book – it was titled 'Nude' by Picasso. 'I've got a picture of a bare woman,' he shouted and he showed us a picture. It showed a roughly crude painting, childlike in its execution of a flat-chested woman whose entire middle section was a large gap. She was painted in cubist style and bore no resemblance to anything we'd ever seen living or dead.

'That's a lousy photo,' said Tomo, holding it upside down to see if it made any more sense. 'She's been eating too many Oxos.'

The next piece in the jigsaw was supplied by Tomo himself – he did a paper round and one day found a copy of a nudist magazine called *Health and Efficiency* inserted by mistake between the leaves of somebody's *Eagle* that he was delivering. It was Tomo's custom to read all the comics on his round as he was travelling along. It meant that he fell off his bike a lot and the morning papers sometimes didn't get delivered until dinnertime, but Tomo reckoned it saved him having to buy them. We sat outside the toffee shop one summer morning, arguing whether six gobstoppers gave you better value for money than a liquorice smoking set, when there was a terrible crash and Tomo lay sprawled in the middle of the road before us, his bike on top of him. We picked him up and carried him back to the curb.

'Look at this, look at this,' he said breathlessly, pointing a trembling finger at the magazine that had fallen open on his knees. It was a photograph of six girls with enormous bosoms on a sandy beach with nothing but a beach ball between them.

Five little erections pointed heavenward.

Bunny ran off, crying, 'I'm turning into stone like my mum said I would!'

'They've got no mickeys,' said Wharfie and he spoke the truth for where the mickeys should have been, if they'd had any, there was nothing but a blank patch. The retoucher's brush had sent into oblivion the only clues we might have had to the question that was puzzling us all.

That night I followed my Grandfather into the kitchen. Looking round to make sure that neither my Mother nor my Grandmother could hear I said, 'Grandad, is it a sin to look at bare ladies?'

'Begob, and no child. Isn't some of de greatest art in de world dat which depicts de human form? Why d'ye ask such a class of question?'

'Because I looked at a picture of a bare lady this morning and my mickey turned to stone.'

'Begob, in Oireland such a ting wouldn't happen till you was tirty years old and den only in extreme circumstances! Choild o'grace, it must be all de red meat you're eatin' in dem school dinners! I tink de time has come for you and me to have a little talk,' and he drew me closer towards him. 'You see, son,' he said, sitting on the mop bucket, 'neither your Grandmother nor meself are going to be here much longer.'

'Are you moving house?' I asked.

'No, but no man can be livin' for ever and de time will soon come for God to call us into heaven.'

I didn't believe him, because he often talked like this – particularly when he was drunk or wanted to borrow money off me. 'And before we leave yer, I wanted to be sure dat yer feet are firmly on de right path. First of all dere's some tings I have to tell yez. Dey may be hard for yez to understand at first, but dis is all part of becoming a man and I wants yez to listen to me carefully now and take what I'm telling yez like a soldier. Will yez do that?'

I said that I would, and proudly stuck my chest out, standing to attention. He looked at me seriously and said, 'Dere's no Fadder Christmas.'

'No Father Christmas—' I reeled back against the kitchen sink, my hand to my forehead.

'And de tooth fairy is a load of mullarkey.'

'Oh no! Not the tooth fairy.'

'We wasn't going to tell yez until yez was eighteen years old but since yer seem to be maturin' so quick I decided to tell yez now.'

'I bet I'm adopted too,' I burst out, prepared for the worst now that my world had been blown apart.

'Adopted, is it? Not at all! Begob, if your poor mother was in de way of adoptin' someting, I tell yer now she'd rather have had a canary or a little dog or a kitten or someting of dat class. No, for good or bad—' and he looked at me sadly, 'you're all ours. But I have to tell yer another ting,' he said, stretching out his legs.

I was prepared for anything now.

'De ting I showed you with de piece of string going in de one ear and out de udder was a trick.'

I slumped down wearily against the draining board. So this was growing up? Nothing was ever going to be the same again. 'I bet you're going to tell me there's no bogey man,' I cried, tears rolling down my cheeks like sledgers on a snowy hill as I waited for yet another member of my pantheon to be ousted.

'Dere is no bogey man,' nodded my Grandad, 'but dere are leprechauns and you can cure warts by rubbing dem on a pig's trotter and it really is unlucky to see two humpty backs on de one day.'

I'd recovered a little now and, leaning on the sink, I wiped my eyes. Strangely I felt different, a little sadder but also as though in some way I'd grown suddenly a little older. I felt

138

that I'd put behind me my childhood.

'So where do babies come from?' I asked firmly.

'I don't know,' he said, 'your Grandmother won't tell me.'

I stared through the window out at the grimy streets and the slate roofs shining in the drizzle. It seemed as though I'd never find the answer to this mystery.

'But I want to tell you dis, now. As you grow up you'll find dere'll be temptations in yer way to smoke and drink and go wid bad companions. Now yez mustn't give in to dose temptations because it will stunt yer growth. Also now when you're lying in bed at night de Devil might come along and whisper in your ear for ye to touch yer mickey. Now if ye do dat you'll go blind and all yer children will be born thin. Here, now, I want yez to read dis,' and he thrust a little book in my hand. 'Don't look at it now, but read it later on,' and he patted me on the head.

'Have yez had yer spends yet?' he asked. I said I had. 'Yer couldn't see yer way to lending me the price of a pint could yer now? Me throat's like the inside of a camel driver's welly.'

That night, by torchlight under the sheets of my bed, I took the book from under my pillow and looked at it. It was a clothbound volume entitled *Things Every Boy Should Know*, while below was the legend 'given free with the *Boy's Own Paper*. For King and Empire 1908.'

I opened it up, and inside in old-fashioned print were the words 'A young boy's guide to health and happiness.' There were some illustrations that showed degenerate Turks on one side of the page and a healthy-looking Englishman playing cricket on the other while below was the caption 'Which would you rather be?'

The first chapter was called 'Personal Hygiene' and went on at some length about always washing between your toes *and other little crannies*. The second chapter, headed 'Self Abuse and Self Denial' hinted darkly at what would happen to you if you 'wasted your energies in the solitary vice that weakens and leads to madness'. At the end of the text was a picture of 'Jojo the dog-faced boy', who was held up as an extreme example of what would happen if boys indulged in this solitary vice, the nature of which was still a mystery to me. 'What is it?' I wondered. I knew what vices were, because I'd seen them in the woodwork room at school. There were a lot of them. Did this mean that if you only had one vice your face went hairy? I read on, and as I read it became clear that what the book was talking about was – mickey touching!

Ye gods! Not only would you go blind and all your children be born thin but you'd end up looking like a Crufts' champion as well! I shone the torch further down the bed and looked at my mickey with horror. I jumped up and, running across the bedroom, looked in the mirror above the dressing-table examining my face by torchlight to see if hairs were sprouting on my cheeks yet. On my top lip there was a fair, soft down. Ye gods! It was happening already and I'd only looked at it.

The last chapter of the book had the heading 'A Happy Union' and showed various sorts of couples hand in hand and embracing chastely and had captions such as 'A life fulfilled', 'A pillar of society', and 'Manning the ship of Empire'. At the end of the chapter was a section entitled 'Mastering The Physical Side of the Marriage Bed' and some diagrams showed you what to do when you were married. It seemed both painful and ludicrous, and I vowed I was never going to have anything to do with it.

The next morning I left the house early and wandered the streets aimlessly, confusion burning in my soul. All the stuff I'd been reading about mickeys and marriage was all related to a subject I knew nothing at all about – girls. It seemed that here somehow was the link between growing up, babies and Jojo the dog-faced boy. I walked further along the street, looking at my reflection in the shop windows and pondering on the mysteries of life. Suddenly my face sprouted hair. I stood fixed to the spot, looking at my reflection in the window. My entire face was covered in thick fur. Then my reflection flicked out a long pink tongue and began licking its balls. It was a cat in the butcher's window. With relief glowing inside me like a hot dinner I turned left into the local park.

On a bench by the drinking fountain and the putting green sat Bernadette McClusky – the jelly baby queen. She was fourteen now and had left our school to go to the local grammar school. I hadn't seen her for a long time and thought, as I looked at her, that she'd changed a lot. Her chest seemed a lot bigger than I remembered it, her hair was longer and her lips were redder.

'Hello,' I said.

'Well, look what the cat's dragged in,' she answered friendlily, moving along the bench to let me sit down. 'You've got a face like a wet weekend.'

'I'm worried about ending up like Jojo the dog-faced boy.'

'Jojo the what?' And I told her how I'd asked my Grandad where babies come from, and how he'd told me of the perils of mickey-touching, and how he'd given me this book with a picture of Jojo the dog-faced boy in it.

'Come here,' she said, taking me by the hand and leading me into the rhododendron bushes. Inside the bushes was a little clearing, private and secluded. Above it the sun shone and birds sang while all around us was a green wall.

She put her jacket down on the grass. 'Lie down,' she said. Who was I to argue? She was bigger than me and went horse riding. I did as I was told.

'Give me your hand,' she said.

'Are you going to read my future?'

'No, stupid – now close your eyes.' I closed my eyes and she put my hand on something warm and soft. 'Is that nice?' she asked. I couldn't answer; my throat was drying up like a swamp edge in the tropical sun, my head was spinning and every drop of blood in my body seemed to be concentrated in one spot.

I opened my mouth to speak. There was a sudden thump and I woke up on the bedroom floor.

'I had a bad dream,' I told my Mother.

'No you didn't,' she said, 'I caught you in the bushes with Bernadette McClusky and if I catch you doing that again I'll kick your backside all the way from here to kingdom come.'

But I did do it again. It was a few years later in the middle of a field of long grass that grew on the only farm we had in our area, a little dairy farm belonging to the local milkman. Bernadette McClusky and I were just coming to the interesting bit when there was a sudden noise as though a giant bumblebee had arrived on the scene. On the far horizon my myopic eyes made out a crimson dot advancing rapidly towards us. 'It's Captain Marvel,' I muttered, half under my breath, but it wasn't. It was Monsignor McGuinness, riding a five-hundred cc Norton motorbike and swinging a thurifer. We dressed hurriedly and with my braces fastened through one leg of her knickers hobbled across the field ahead of him. Strangely, he never got any closer to us than when I first saw him. We rearranged our clothes and as we stumbled hunch-backed with unspent passion down the warm country lane towards home, he changed into a clump of rosebay willow-herb and floated away like thistledown on the wind.

Suddenly something above us caught my attention. We looked up at the sky.

'It's a flying saucer,' said Bernadette McClusky.

'No,' I said sadly, 'it's a canoe.'

I knew then that my life was to change utterly and for ever, for in the canoe were my Grandmother and Grandfather and as

they floated higher above us, ascending slowly into heaven, my Grandfather waved at me and smiled, and my Grandmother leaned over the side of the canoe and shouted words which have since become graven on my heart.

'Remember two things, Mícheál ó Mo Chroí – God is a heavy drinker, and yer mickey gets you into nuthin' but trouble.'